FORTUNE-TELL

A fascinating practical guide to the ancient art of casting the runes.

In this series

FORTUNE-TELLING BY DICE
David and Julia Line

FORTUNE-TELLING BY PLAYING CARDS
Nerys Dee

FORTUNE-TELLING BY TAROT CARDS
Jo Logan

FORTUNE-TELLING BY RUNES

A Guide to Casting and Interpreting the Ancient European Rune Stones

by

DAVID AND JULIA LINE

THE AQUARIAN PRESS
Wellingborough, Northamptonshire

First published 1984

© DAVID AND JULIA LINE 1984

British Library Cataloguing in Publication Data

Line, David
    Fortune telling by runes,
    1. Fortune telling by runes
    I. Title   II. Line, Julia
    133.3'3   BF1891.R/

    ISBN 0-85030-367-2

Printed and bound in Great Britain

CONTENTS

		Page
Introduction		7
Chapter		
1.	Introducing Runes	9
2.	Runes – The Background	14
3.	What You Need for Casting Runes	22
4.	Casting and Reading Runes	29
5.	Sample Casts	33
6.	Freya's Eight	48
7.	Hagal's Eight	62
8.	Tiu's Eight	74
9.	Skjebne	89
	Bibliography	91
	Suppliers	93
	Index	95

To T.W.L., without whom the authors would not have been possible.

INTRODUCTION

What does the future hold in store for me? This is the 64,000 dollar question which mankind has been asking itself for countless centuries.

Possibly to obey the laws of supply and demand, various different cultures have independently assembled ways and means to attempt to answer that question. At the same time, these cultures have spawned their soothsayers, seers, prophets, village wise women and so on – all exponents in the art of divination. Today, the prophecies of Nostradamus are still avidly read, you can still find palmists at the end of the pier and horoscopes seem to be an essential component of magazines and popular national newspapers.

Casting runes to shed light on the future is one of the least well documented methods of divination and it is ironic that this wholly European discipline should, in Europe, fall behind Oriental I Ching and Middle Eastern Tarot.

But, divinatory methods apart, any activity which offers the chance to gain knowledge of the future without the backing of logical rationalization, scientific proof or experimental repeatibility, loses one supremely important advantage: credibility. The credibility of divination often results from no more than a personal observation backed by a positive desire to believe – something which is all too easily undone by practitioners of the art who are either charlatans or outrageous egoists, ill-informed dabblers or members of the lunatic fringe.

In the same way that many ufologists, clairvoyants, and so on, are their own worst enemies by trying to rationalize the irrational with bogus psychology, quasi-science and fluent patter, so too are some diviners.

The act of casting runes can be *seen*. The relationship between the stones and their respective meanings can be observed in operation. But the uncanny knack they have of being right, for the greater part of the time, cannot be explained in purely factual terms. Rational theories can and are applied – but they still remain only theories.

At the end of the day you will either believe in runes or not, especially if you easily relate to the results of a cast and what it has to say. The only hope for some degree of explanation lies in the future and is best illustrated with this analogy:

Three hundred years ago, a man travelling at night across the marshlands of eastern England might well have seen a ghostly, flickering light dancing above the boggy ground. There would be no doubt in his mind that he had witnessed yet another appearance of Will o' the Wisp, an evil spirit whose sole aim was to lure travellers such as himself to a grim death in the treacherous marshes.

Will o' the Wisp can still be seen today, but our modern traveller would be more amused than alarmed. After all, the apparition is nothing more sinister than spontaneously burning marsh gas – methane, generated by rotting vegetation in the bog.

These two sightings, separated by three hundred years, do not change the nature of what is observed – it was burning marsh gas then just as it is burning marsh gas today. While both observers would have witnessed the same phenomena, the difference lies in its interpretation. One is based on known, proven scientific fact, the other on superstition and cant. What our ancient traveller saw really did exist, and he observed it accurately. But his conclusion about what caused the image was utterly wrong.

In a similar way we can accurately observe runes in action. We should, however, be cautious about the explanations we offer for the phenomena in case we create another 'Will o' the Wisp', ripe for scoffing at in years to come.

When the enigma of runes is resolved, we hope that the observations in this book remain correct.

D. & J. L.
Blofield

1

INTRODUCING RUNES

This is essentially a practical book, containing all the information needed to cast rune stones and to interpret individual and group meanings from where the stones fall on a runic chart. Runes are an alternative to I Ching, Tarot and even tea-leaves and, in many respects, offer significant advantages over their oriental, middle eastern and home-brewed counterparts.

Runes are basically a practical method of fortune-telling and reflect, to some degree, their northern European origins. They are easier to interpret than I Ching and compared with Tarot cards, require less intuitive application by the reader. And, unlike tea-leaves, runes do not demand an artistic eye to achieve a meaning, although the pattern or order in which they fall has a direct bearing on results.

The danger with any form of divination is that it is often regarded as mere 'fortune-telling' and therefore is either instantly dismissed or ignored, before asking the question how does it 'work'?

Perhaps the easiest rationalization would be to simply quote Carl Jung, who claimed there is a positive psychic link between mankind and the environment. He qualified this further by explaining that it was this psychic relationship which accounted for all those odd coincidences and happenings which take place in the lives of most men, women and children at some time. Jung's label for these was 'synchronistic events' and led him to investigate many forms of divination.

The implications of this are that there is no such thing in life as an accident and that there are too many positive influences at work to make anything the result of mere chance. The selection of a particular group of rune stones, or Tarot cards, or the picking up of a particular numeric sequence of yarrow sticks is not luck but some deep subconscious form of judgement.

If this is the case, what do runes tell the reader? Certainly they do not portray specific future events. What they do show are probable future trends based on existing circumstances – something very different altogether. It is this assessment of the current scene which enables the querent to cope with and understand both existing circumstances and the likely results of his or her actions.

With the knowledge of what is possible, the querent may then have an opportunity to apply some direction to his or her course through life.

The 'ifs', 'ands' and 'buts' of divination are endless and it is only too easy to get bogged down by dogma or cynicism and still not achieve a philosophically acceptable answer.

Runes should be kept very much in perspective. They are the means to an end, not the end in themselves. These 'tools' cannot be attributed with mystical powers of their own – although there is no doubt that they have been in the past – nor can the symbols or characters with which runes are inscribed be given their own magical properties. Runic characters are really a form of shorthand, with each one carrying a meaning. When a group of runes is assessed, the shorthand meanings combine to form an overall picture – a complete sentence.

It is the hand of the querent which selects a particular group of runes and it is the same hand which casts them on the cloth. The story, the meanings, perhaps even the 'magic' is within the querent, not within the stones.

Many forms of divination are accompanied by some form of ritual. It may be the way a cloth is laid, the seating position of the querent, even the level of lighting used during a reading. In some cases it might be exhortations spoken aloud such as 'This is his hopes and fears' as one Tarot card is laid down upon another.

There is little value in this – certainly no magical or occult significance, but the effects of order and repetitiveness, part and parcel of ritual, might, for some, aid concentration. Treat ritual with caution, the more complex and convoluted it becomes the more it could be used to disguise ineptitude, even charlatanism.

To recap, perhaps the best analogy for runes is to think of the sailor at sea. He has his chart showing coastlines and waters, navigational buoys and beacons. He knows where he has come from and where he wants to go, but all the time his voyage is being affected by the wind and the tide, not always to his advantage. He uses tools – compass, dividers, parallel rules, radio, echo sounders and a myriad of other items – to help him establish his position and plot the next leg of his course to his destination.

At the risk of waxing too lyrical, runes can be compared to the navigator's instruments. They are tools enabling the querent to plot his or her position at the moment when the stones are cast and then to take positive action to continue safely on the journey – this time through life.

Other aspects of 'runes' can be seen in the following extract from a Norse poem, the 'Volsunga Saga', in which Brynhild teaches Sigurd runic application.

Runes of war know thou
If great thou will be!
Cut them on hilt of hardened sword,
Some on the brand's back,
Some on its shining side,
Twice the name Tyr therein.

Sea-runes good at need,
Learnt for ship's saving,
For the good health of the swimming-horse;
On the stern cut them,
Cut them on the rudder-blade
And set flame the shaven oar:
Howso big be the sea-hills,
Howso blue beneath,
Hail, from the main then comest thou home.

Word-runes learn well
If thou wilt that no man
Pay back grief for the grief thou gavest;
Wind thou these,
Weave thou these,
Cast thou these all about thee,
At the Thing,
Where folk throng,
Until the full doom faring.

Of ale-runes know the wisdom
If thou wilt that another's wife
Should not bewray thine heart that trusteth;
Cut them on the mead-horn,

On the back of each hand,
And nick an N upon thy nail.

Help-runes shalt thou gather
If skill thou wouldst gain
To loosen child from low-laid mother;
Cut they be in hands hollow,
Wrapped the joints round about,
Call for the good folks' gainsome helping.

Learn the bough-runes' wisdom
If leech-lore thou lovest;
And wilt wot about wounds' searching
On the bark they be scored;
On the buds of trees
Whose boughs look eastwards ever.

Thought-runes shalt thou deal with
If thou wilt be of all men
Fairest-souled wight, and wisest,
These areded
These first-cut
These first took to heart high Hropt.

On the shield were they scored
That stands before the shining God,
On early-waking's oar,
On all-knowing's hoof,
On the wheel which runneth
Under Rögnir's chariot;
On Sliepnir's jaw-teeth,
On the sleigh's traces,
On the rough bear's paws,
And on Bragi's tongue,
On the wolf's claws,
And on eagle's bill,
On bloody wings,
And bridge's end,
On loosing palms,
And pity's path:

On glass, on gold,

And on goodly silver,
In wine and in wort,
And the seat of the witch-wife;
On Gungnir's point,
And Grani's bosom;
On the Norn's nail,
And the neb of the night-owl.

All these so-cut
Were shaven and sheared,
And mingled with holy mead,
And sent upon wide ways enow,
Some abide with the elves,
Some abide with the AEsir,
Or with the wise Vanir,
Or some still hold the sons of mankind.

These be the book-runes,
And the runes of good-help,
And all the ale-runes,
And the runes of much might;
To whomso they may avail,
Unbewildered unspoilt;
They are wholesome to have:
Thrive thou with these them.
When thou hast learnt their lore,
Till the Gods end thy life-days.

2

RUNES – THE BACKGROUND

'Just a few pieces of stone with symbols on them – that's how many people regard runes, associating them, perhaps, with ancient northern European cultures and some obscure branch of occultism, but crediting them with little else.

Opinions vary as to the original purpose of runic symbols. Were they a form of alphabet for pre-Christian tribes in northern Europe and the British Isles or were they developed only for use in ancient magical rites?

In later years the word 'rune' came to mean a spell or poem, yet many experts believe that runes were simply a convenient alphabet for secular documents, legal records and contracts. There is no sure evidence of a wide literary use of runes in very early times. A few runic manuscripts have survived, but most of these come from a later period.

Curiously, the word 'rune' is derived from two roots: the Germanic 'ru' and the Gothic 'runa' – two related forms which mean mystery, secret and secrecy. Does this endorse their original usage, reinforcing the secrecy and mystery of both secular and legal matters? One only has to look at the legal jargon of today to see that it is carefully contrived to make understanding by lay people no easy task. Or did this association with mystery and secrecy refer to something much deeper and much older?

Certainly runic characters have not taken on their shapes – combinations of straight and angular lines – for any particular symbolic reason. There is no cause to doubt that they developed in this way because it was easiest and most practical for letters to be carved in wood, always in such a way that the single lines did not follow the grain and thus weaken the timber 'tablet'. Straight line characters were also eminently suitable for carving on stone and bone – even metal.

But even such a simple concept as an alphabet composed of a series of straight and angled lines cannot remain simple for long. As with the development of different languages and, in turn, regional dialects, so runic characters evolved into numerous patterns. Like today's world languages, runes can be categorized into major groups and, for convenience, fall into three main categories.

The basic Germanic series of runic symbols can be found on about a hundred inscriptions believed to date from the third to the eighth centuries AD. This alphabet was called a Futhork, and just as the word 'alphabet' took the first two letters from the Greek, so runes took 'futhork' from the first six letters: F, U, TH, O, R, and K. This runic alphabet was divided into three groups each comprising eight characters, giving a total of twenty-four characters in all. Known as 'aettir', these basic divisions were sometimes named after Norse deities: Freya's eight, Hagal's eight and Tiu's eight.

Each runic character had a dual meaning – outwardly material, and inwardly spiritual. It is these runic symbols on which the divinations in this book are based.

Freya's Eight

ᚡ *feoh*, cattle or fee

ᚢ *ur*, yore or ox

ᚦ *thorn*, *thurs*, thorn or giant

ᚩ *oss*, Asa, god

ᚱ *rit*, sunwheel, sun-wain

ᚲ *kaon*, torch, life-strength

ᚷ *gifu*, blessing, gift

ᚹ *wunna*, bliss, Woden

Hagal's eight

ᚺ *hagal*, hail, health

ᚾ *naut*, need

ᛁ *is*, ice

ᛇ *yer*, year, harvest

ᛉ *yr*, yewtree

ᛈ *peorth*, paddock, berg

ᛦ *aquizi*, stone axe

ᛋ *sig*, sun, winning

Tiu's eight

ᛏ *tiu*, the god Tiu

ᛚ *lagu*, lake, water of life

ᛒ *birca*, birch tree, berg   ◇ *ing*, kin, offspring

ᛗ *eh*, *eoh*, horse, steed   ᛦ *odal*, homeland, holding

ᛗ *man*, mankind, world   ᛞ *dag*, day

The Runes

It is safe to assume that each rune corresponded to what is now accepted as the gutteral sound of German. There was not the scope, however, to convey the more resonant vowel sounds of our pre-Norman Anglo-Saxon language and, in order to cope, the number of characters in the futhork increased first to twenty-eight and then later to thirty-one. This Anglo-Saxon variety of runes is believed to have appeared around the fifth century AD in the British Isles.

As with all languages and scripts, changes continued, especially in phonetic values. Two of the old Anglo-Saxon characters – 'thorn' and 'wynn' – were adopted by the old English alphabet while the third rune, 'th', was used in early English script to supplement our own familiar alphabet. Through careless calligraphy it came to resemble the letter 'y' and yet retained the sound 'th'. Today we can see the remnants of this in such antique signs as 'Ye Olde Englyshe Teashoppe'.

The third major subdivision of runes belongs to Scandinavia. Here the reverse happened and the parallel linguistic development of Scandinavian languages resulted in the number of runes being reduced to a mere sixteen characters.

So we have a very straightforward account of runic development – nothing very mysterious or secret, just a simple alphabet. But there's usually two sides to any story: let's look at the other.

According to ancient Norse legend and described in the Icelandic poem 'The Elder Edda', the god Odin (or Woden) was the original master of the runes. The story goes that in order to rediscover the already existing secret of the runes, Odin was submitted to the barbaric and painful ordeal of being hung upside-down on a gallows for nine nights as a sacrifice. The gallows in this context are synonymous with the sacred Ash Tree of Nordic mythology, Yggdrasil. The meaning of the word 'Yggdrasil' can be interpreted in three ways and, as Bill Butler says in *The Definitive Tarot*, the gallows, rood and tree are all Yggdrasil – The World Tree.

Whether or not Odin was a god or just a warrior king, the

rediscovery of the runes is, in legend, attributed to him. Legend also tells us that Odin's eight-legged horse, Sleipnir, had runic symbols carved on his teeth. It is equally worth noting that all Anglo-Saxon kings claimed descendency from Odin and, in pre-Norman times it was a necessary 'qualification' for kingship to be of his blood.

The twelfth card in the major arcana of the Tarot pack illustrates, perhaps by coincidence, the sacrifice to which Odin subjected himself in order to regain the knowledge of the runes. The symbolic components of this card point towards the theory of spiritual enlightenment through suffering – a principle adopted by many religions.

Curiously, there is a link – perhaps coincidental – with Tarot cards and the twelfth card of the major Arcana, the Hanged Man, which symbolizes the dying god. Regardless of the difference between packs, this particular card contains the same pictorial components. We see a man hanged by one foot, the free leg crossed at right angles to the other and the arms positioned behind his back to form the hint of a triangle. The symbolism of a triangle surmounted by a cross represents the descent of light into darkness in order to achieve redemption. (This has parallels in many Christian teachings.) In short, it represents redemption or spiritual awakening through suffering – just as Odin discovered the runes through personal sacrifice. This link between Odin and the Hanged Man is illustrated in the following extracts from the translation by Paul B. Taylor and W. H. Auden of 'The Words of the High One from The Elder Edda' (*The Elder Edda: A Selection,* Faber & Faber, 1973).

> Wounded I hung on a wind-swept gallows
> For nine long nights,
> Pierced by a spear, pledged to Odin,
> Offered, myself to myself;
> The wisest know not from whence spring
> The roots of that ancient rood.
>
> They gave me no bread, they gave me no mead;
> I looked down; with a loud cry
>
> I took up runes; from that tree I fell.
>
> and:
>
> I know a twelfth: if a tree bear
> A man hanged in a halter,
> I can carve and stain strong runes
> That will cause the corpse to speak
> Reply to whatever I ask.

The runes as a means of divination are not well documented, although some academic works have been published on the historic origins. We know that the spread of Christianity, via the Roman Church, to the outermost parts of Europe, brought with it the essence of the alphabet we use today. The pagan use of runes for purposes of divination was outlawed by the Church and categorized as 'a tool of the devil'. Although the Church actively tried to stamp out runic divination, it continued to be practised in secret and became inevitably linked with witches, warlocks and their arts.

Runes, both esoteric and practical, continued to be studied throughout history until this century and nowhere else were they held in such high esteem as Germany. Runes became a vital component of the Third Reich's belief in Aryan superiority. From the theory of the Urrunen - an ancient north German script and the forerunner of the runes as we know them - the Nazis tried to prove that this alphabet was the root from which all others developed - Phoenician, Greek and so on. With this theory, another coal was added to the fire of the Nazi's belief in Aryan racial superiority. But, as with the way that the Third Reich tried to prove a racial link between themselves and their allies, the Japanese, this idea should not be considered seriously.

Nevertheless, runic associations with Nazi Germany only served once again to bring runes into some vague disrepute as they had once been when linked with witchcraft.

Another illustration of how runes were adopted by Hitler's Germany was in the way that the SS used the runic form of ⚡ as symbols for their collar badges. The letter, ⚡ 'Sig', also stands for victory - which is something they achieved, albeit briefly. But we must not forget that runes, like the swastika, are very ancient symbols which were in use long before Hitler appropriated them.

Runes had another outlet still: they were used on perpetual calendars known in Norway as Primstaves and in Denmark as Rimstocks. These precursors of the Staffordshire clog almanacs were timber or bone tablets or rings bearing characters representing the days of the year, the prime or golden numbers and seasonal symbols.

Clog almanacs were still in use in this country at the end of the seventeenth century and have been well documented by Dr Plot in his book *A Natural History of Staffordshire* (E. J. Morton, 1973). These clog almanacs were similar to the earlier runic primstaves and were constructed from oblong lengths of wood, brass, bone or horn, marked with notches representing the days of the months of the year on each of the four edges. Flanking left and right were symbols indicating the lunar cycle, saint's days and so on. They could be hung on a wall, stood on the mantlepiece and even carried in a pocket.

Two artifacts – a ring and a mount – which are adorned with runic inscriptions.
They were found beside the Thames and can now be seen in the British
Museum, along with numerous other examples of the runic art.

Another unusual runic link is with our old currency: pounds, shillings and pence. The solidus was a Roman silver coin which bore a runic inscription and was still in use in this country until the seventh century. Our £sd originates from the Roman coins of libra (£), solidus (s) and denarius (d), so even today runes still have some connection with day-to-day life.

There are still many fine examples of runic inscriptions to be seen both in this country and abroad, in museums and in their original settings. One such example is the Frank's Casket dated about AD 650-700. The right side is in the Museo Nazionale del Bargello in Florence and the rest can be seen in the British Museum. The Hunterston brooch, now in Edinburgh, was marked with runes in the tenth century, perhaps by Norse settlers in Man, which has yielded twenty-four inscribed crosses. There are runes on the Collingham stone in Yorkshire (seventh century) and the Bewcastle Cross in Cumberland; the Ruthwell Cross in Dunfriesshire is somewhat later. Other runic inscriptions can be seen in Ireland, Wales, Devon, Cornwall, Silchester and Scotland. In Denmark and Schleswig there are over fifty inscriptions dating from the third to the sixth century and in Norway over sixty such inscriptions dating from the fifth to the eighth century. Manuscripts are rare and relatively late but examples may be seen in the British Museum.

3

WHAT YOU NEED
FOR CASTING RUNES

The basic tools you will need for runic divination are a set of 25 rune stones and a casting cloth. There are 24 stones inscribed with runic symbols and one blank stone. While this might appear complex and expensive to set up, this is in fact not so. In its basic form your set of rune stones could simply be twenty-five dominoes with runic symbols drawn or painted on the reverse sides. The runic cloth needs to be no more than a sheet of ordinary paper big enough to carry a 10" (230mm) diameter circle.

Serious practitioners of runic divination are likely to go to greater lengths in their production or purchase of runes and runic cloths. Examples of runes produced in timber, terracotta and porcelain are shown on these pages along with more flamboyant designs for the cloths which can, of course, be adapted to suit individual needs but, in principle, must contain common essential components. Sources for purchasing craftsman-made rune stones and cloths are given at the end of this book.

The basic runic cloth, or casting cloth, consists of a sheet of paper or material onto which are drawn or sewn three concentric circles. Working on the basis that the runes themselves will measure about 1" x 1" (25mm x 25mm), the ideal diameters for the three circles are 3", 7", and 10" (75mm, 178mm and 254mm). In no way should these measurements be treated as absolutes – they are only general guides.

From the three circles you can see that four areas are created: the inner circle, middle circle, outer circle and the space beyond. Each of these areas is significant in determining the meaning of runes as they fall across the cloth.

The centre circle is called 'skjebne' – the Norwegian word for destiny. In other philosophies the term 'karma' could possibly apply but this implies that, while fate is not haphazard and subject to chance, it is determined by an individual's actions in previous lives or spiritual conditions. While one might subscribe to the principle of 'destiny', its associations with 'past lives' isn't necessarily acceptable.

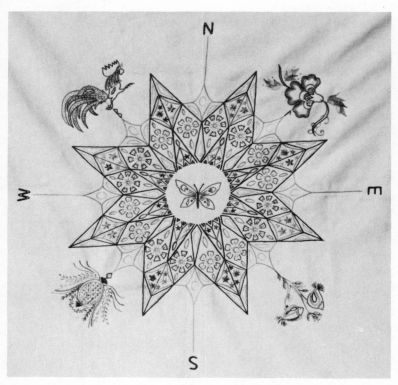

Many practitioners of runic divination will adapt the basic pattern for the runic cloth to suit their own purposes. This flamboyant design still retains the essential 'areas' of the simple concentric circle design. But more elaborate symbolism is used here and the reader will need a keener eye to identify the exact location of cast stones. This is not recommended for the novice.

The middle ring is known as 'outside skjebne', while the outer ring is divided into four segments, each with its own attributions. In broad terms, working outwards from the centre of the runic cloth, the circles take the querent from purely spiritual matters to those of a more immediate emotional or physical nature.

Various labels can be applied to the outer four segments. Some students of runic divination nominate the segments under the headings of health, home, wealth and success, but in practice such bald and obvious labels can often only serve to confuse the results of a cast. Other alternatives in use are the equally obvious division of earth, air, fire and water, conjuring the symbolism of alchemy which again is capable of causing some confusion when interpreting results. Another fallacious system – this time incorporating the runes themselves – is to apply astrological symbols and significance to both cloth and stones. As the use of alchemic elements remains popular, we have retained them in the explanatory chapters but added them to the more appropriate symbols.

In fact, the labels for the outer circle segments should simply be a means to identify the spaces relative to one another and the angle

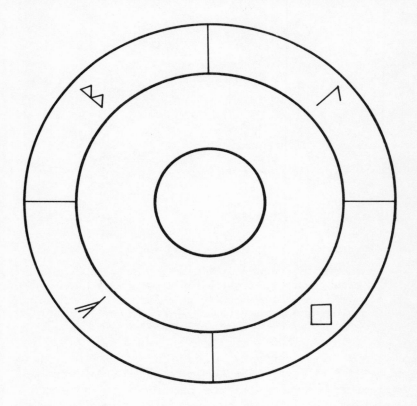

The basic casting cloth comprises three concentric circles. The outer area is segmented and a rune stone can land on any one of seven possible locations – each determining a specific meaning for the rune in question.

from which the runes were cast. The significance of the segments is primarily dependent upon the nature of the stones which land on them.

To this end, the simple runic system of labelling is least likely to cause confusion. These are 'Feoh' (Ⱶ), 'Birca' (ᛒ), 'Ing' (◇) and 'Lagu' (ᚱ).

By dividing the outer circle into four segments, the cloth offers the option of seven possible 'landing sites': skjebne, outside skjebne, Feoh, Birca, Ing, Lagu and outside the runic circle. It is

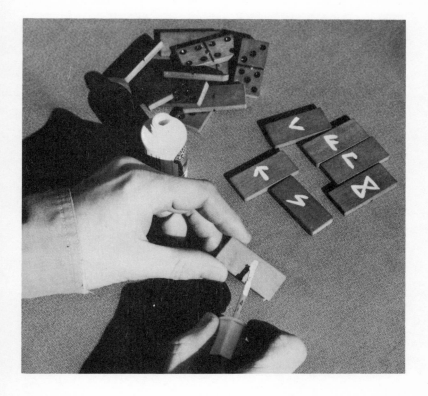

The quickest and easiest way to produce a set of rune stones is to paint or draw runic symbols on the back of a set of dominoes. Here correcting fluid is being used but chinagraph, ink, felt tip or even enamel paint can be used.

interesting to note that the number seven has long been thought to hold substantial occult significance. Hippocrates said that because of its occult virtues number seven has a tendency to bring all things into being. There is also an association between seven and the image of Odin suggested in the twelfth card of the Tarot major arcana which was described in a previous chapter. Here the symbol for seven is the same as the symbolic components of 'The Hanged Man' (Odin) – a triangle above a square. All the sides add up to seven.

Also, perhaps coincidentally, the rune stones themselves have an association with the number seven. By applying the rules of numerology and adding together the digits of 25 – the number of stones used – you arrive at seven: $2 + 5 = 7$.

It is likely that, originally, the runic casting cloth had such positive occult components designed into it. But beware of trying to extract too much symbolic meaning from the relationships of the three basic circles and the four segments.

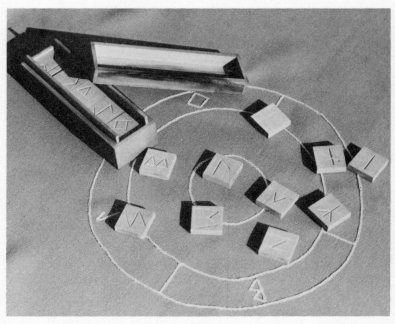

This set of boxed runes has been professionally made using 'pear'. The stones are ideally sized at 1″ x 1″ x ¼″ and the symbols have been lightly carved into the surface of the wood. Other appropriate timbers are oak, elm, ash, yew, rosewood and birch. This set was produced by Michael Westgate.

The casting cloth in its simplest form can be a sheet of paper, and the runes can be as easily manufactured. As already suggested, dominoes with the runic letters painted on the reverse side will serve the purpose. Even if the prospect of carving symbols into wood is a deterrent, there is no great problem in drawing runic letters onto 'stones' cut from a length of inexpensive batten.

As the runic querent has to select and then hold nine runes from the total of twenty-five, prior to casting, the size of rune stones is critical. Runes measuring 1″ x 1″ x ¼″ (25mm x 25mm x 6mm) are recommended as the optimum size. While material thinner than ¼″ (6mm) can be used, it reduces the possibility of runes landing on edge – which in itself is significant to an interpretation.

Although runes made from pine or ramin are adequate, they do not have the same intrinsic quality and 'weight' as those cut from elm, walnut, oak and other more appropriate timbers. The wooden set illustrated in this book has been made from pear – even more esoteric!

Rune stones can be produced in a variety of materials. Those on the left are made from terracotta and are roughly moulded. They certainly give a 'stonelike' feel, are heavy and very durable. The stones on the right are made from porcelain and are shown before final glazing and firing. Here the symbols will be picked out in a second colour. These stones are very smooth to the touch.

All the Northern European trees known to the followers of Odin had their own magical qualities. It would therefore be inappropriate for the serious runic diviner to use such timbers as African or South American mahogany, teak, afrormosia and iroko, all of which, in realistic terms, are perfectly suitable for the job, but would probably not have been known then.

Since neither Letraset nor Meccanorma produce instant rub-down runic lettering, the job must be done by free-hand. As runes consist only of straight lines the work does not require any great calligraphic skills and pleasing results can be achieved with Indian Ink, felt tip pen or even black paint.

For the more adventurous who intend to carve the letters into the wooden stones, two sharp chisels measuring ½″ (12mm) and ¼″ (6mm) will be all that is needed. Here it's a good idea to first draw the letters onto the stones, making sure that they are centred and not too close to the edges. With straight grain softwoods there is a risk of splitting the timber. Simply cut into the wood at an angle of about 45° from each side of the drawn lines to achieve a 'V' shaped cut. If you wish, the carved letters can then be painted in and the stones finished in clear varnish. Remember that one stone – skjebne – is left blank.

4

CASTING AND READING RUNES

Amongst the many advantages runes are claimed to have over Tarot, I Ching and other methods of divination, is the fact that casting and reading is an uncomplicated and relatively speedy process.

With the casting cloth laid out on a suitable surface – a table top, tray or board – the diviner spreads out the stones and shuffles them face down in much the same way as you would for dominoes. From the twenty-five stones the querent selects nine and shuffles these around in cupped hands. When the querent is ready, he or she simply casts the nine stones over the cloth. At this stage it is a good idea to point out that runes are not cast with the vim and vigour of a spin bowler. The action is almost akin to pouring them from an upturned hand with just enough impetus to scatter the runes over the cloth.

Why select only nine stones – why indeed? Some diviners stick to the traditional eleven while others determine the number of stones the querent selects by applying rules of numerology. There are no hard and fast rules here but practice has shown that nine stones can be held in even the smallest hand and provide sufficient numbers to produce a detailed and worthwhile reading.

Another reason for using nine stones with, perhaps, a more appealing justification takes us again to the legend of Odin hanging on Yggdrasill, the World Ash. Here it took nine nights for Odin to gather the knowledge of the runes so, in turn, in order for the querent to gain his knowledge, nine stones should be thrown: one for each night.

Any application of numerology should be treated with some caution. Numerology is, after all, a method of divination far removed from the geographic and cultural origins of runes. It could be argued that applying any aspect of numerology to runes is like trying to mix oil and water. Nevertheless some exponents claim success in this direction, so it is worth giving some mention to this system of stone selection. The number/letter associations used are as follows:

1	2	3	4	5	6	7	8
A	B	C	D	E	U	O	F
I	K	G	M	H	V	Z	P
Q	R	L	T	N	W		
J	S			X			
Y							

The above system, generally favoured by numerologists, is based on the Hebrew alphabet with some assistance from the Greek. The number nine is omitted as it was believed to be the numeral equivalent of the nine lettered name of God and the letters are not listed in the normal order.

Here the diviner locates those numbers corresponding to each letter in the querent's name and, along with the birthdate, adds them together from left to right. All the compound numbers are added together until a single total is reached.

The following example illustrates how a diviner would allocate the number of stones to be selected by John Smith born on the 2nd November 1958.

J O H N   S M I T H   2. 11.   1958
1+7+5+5   +3+4+1+4+5   +2+1+1+1+9+5+8 = 62 = 8 stones

Once the runes have been cast, the diviner must look for a number of key patterns made by the falling stones along with those stones which fall face down or on edge. Although this might outwardly appear difficult it is really just a matter of detailed observation.

More often than not a large proportion of stones will fall together in a clump, some overlapping, some just touching and others very close together. These stones are of prime importance and refer to the most immediate concerns or problems of the querent. The diviner must also gauge the 'order' in which they fell to arrive at the appropriate sequence for reading. Apart from paying close attention to the stones at the moment they are cast, sequences within a group can generally be numbered from the point nearest to the querent outwards.

In some cases an obvious 'progression' of stones will be observed by the diviner – not close enough to each other to warrant labelling as a group but, nonetheless, forming a discernible pattern. A progression can also be generated by a series of stones which have closely linked meanings. Sometimes it will be the sequence of meanings rather than a physical pattern which will indicate a progression.

Secondary groups – perhaps consisting of only two or three stones – can fall in the same cast. These are exactly as the name implies; secondary in importance to the main group. Other stones will scatter singly across the cloth. Again, their initial value is as would appear – one-offs or isolated events but still relevant to the querent.

Stones which fall face down indicate that the meanings are hidden to the querent's conscious mind. They refer to unseen events in the past, present or future which could have a direct bearing on the querent's situation – for good or bad depending on the meaning of the stone and its position on the cloth. They often serve to provide the missing link to something about which the querent is only half aware.

Occasionally runes will land on edge. The simple interpretation for this is that whatever the stone represents, the result could go either way. If a rune lands on edge within an obvious bunch or group, then its position relative to the others and its place on the casting cloth must be noted with special care.

With the position of each rune observed, its attitude and relationship to other groups and single stones noted, the diviner can begin to assemble overall meanings.

If you imagine that each rune is like an isolated word in a sentence, you can see that, in order to complete the sentence, each rune must be fully identified and its meaning interpreted in the light of all the other stones. It's rather like constructing a correct sentence when you know all of the nouns and none of the verbs. For this a small degree of intuition helps but, like mastering any art, it is practice which counts in the end.

Things are made easier by the fact that runes are each allocated a label giving a generic meaning, one which stays with the stone no matter where it falls. This is the key meaning which identifies the nature of the rune and the area in which it operates. The generic meaning is backed up with seven specific meanings, each determined by where the stone falls on the cloth. The only exception here is the rune Hagal – not a good stone to throw!

Combining generic and specific meanings to achieve a particular image or meaning for one stone is straightforward. But remember that with a group of stones, this result must be aligned and related to the others. You must therefore grasp the broad picture painted by all the runes based on 'isolated' compounds.

All the meanings are given in later chapters of this book and, because there are so many ambiguities in the English language, various possible, and still appropriate, alternatives are given to help you tie the meanings of individual stones together.

One final and important point is that not all stones will fall neatly into one of the seven allocated 'slots'. Some will be half in one area and half in another, perhaps with only just a corner of a stone across a border. In cases like these the meaning of a rune in a dual position must be considered carefully and the reading adjusted according to how much of the rune falls into another section. This is best illustrated by example.

If the rune Ing (◇) which affects direct family, falls half in Skjebne (change leading to improvement) and half into outside Skjebne (move of house) this would indicate that by moving home the querent and his family will benefit, perhaps by gaining more space, or in terms of health in a better environment, or they would just get on better generally in a different place.

If the rune Naut (⼂), which is a warning, falls mainly in the Lagu section (⼁) (refusals) with just a corner in outside Skjebne (patience) the probable interpretation would be that plans which the querent is making will be turned down. However, there is just a little hint of encouragement not to give up, to keep at it; that all is not completely lost as it would have been if the rune was entirely in the Lagu section.

5

SAMPLE CASTS

Probably the most practical way to illustrate how to read runes is by example and, for this reason, we have detailed six genuine casts showing where the runic stones landed and how they were interpreted.

While the names of the querents have been changed – for obvious reasons – other details remain true.

On each of the drawings shown note the arrow which indicates the direction from which the stones were cast and the grey shading of stones indicates those which landed face down. The stones are numbered in casting order.

FIGURE 1

Name: Nicola
Age: 32
Occupation: Craftswoman
Background: Currently involved in setting up a new pottery but supported by only a small private income. A new emotional attachment is also very much in mind at the moment.

Major progression: Stones 1-5

1. Yer in Lagu and outside Skjebne: This points to a period of setting up when little in the way of results are forthcoming.

2. Odal in and outside Skjebne: It will be some time before her work is recognized but she must still work hard. There could also be problems over property or legacies.

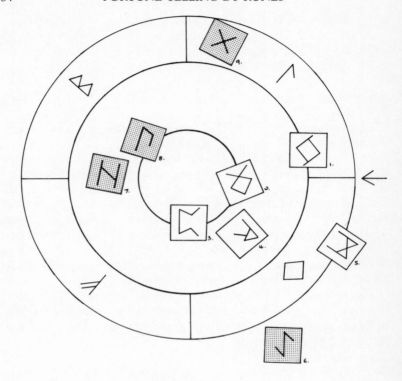

FIGURE 1

3. Peorth in and outside Skjebne: Her new found sexuality and emotional involvement could do more harm than good as far as work is concerned. Probably only a pleasant distraction but the querent is reading too much into it. She would be advised to turn it to her own good.

4. Rit outside Skjebne: This reinforces the idea that success can only come through her own efforts and that work must be treated very seriously. It could result in travel.

5. Man in Ing and outside the circle: Not everyone is on her side. She must keep her ears and eyes open for any signs of deceit.

Progression summary: Work must come first and foremost and should be taken very seriously in order to succeed. She should avoid distractions and be prepared for unexpected obstacles.

6. Single stone – Yr face down outside the circle: This indicates that she could create health problems in the search for her ambition. It could equally apply to her emotional attachment or work or the conflict between the two.

Secondary progression: Stones 7 and 8

7. Hagal outside Skjebne: Disruptions are indicated over which she has no control or indeed knowledge.

8. Ur mostly outside but also slightly into Skjebne: Distant influences could be beneficial but she must be prepared to respond quickly to new opportunities.

Progression summary: Things are happening behind the scenes which could bring improvement – even though, on the face of it, this might not seem the case. She should be prepared to act quickly.

9. Single stone – Gifu in Lagu: This points towards a joint venture as being one way to achieve success.

Cast summary
Nicola will not achieve success overnight. Whatever happens it will involve considerable singlemindedness, determination and hard work. There will be a variety of obstacles and distractions in the way and these will need to be put into perspective and treated accordingly. Many of the immediate problems could be solved by thinking about joint activities or a partnership.

Result
Nicola has allowed emotional distractions to interfere with her work. At the time of writing her business venture is not coming up to expectation.

FIGURE 2

Name: Geoffrey
Age: 35
Occupation: Engineer
Background: Lives on a houseboat with wife and four children.

Recently sold up business with intention of moving abroad. Has spent considerable amount of time and money to refurbish boat in order to take it abroad.

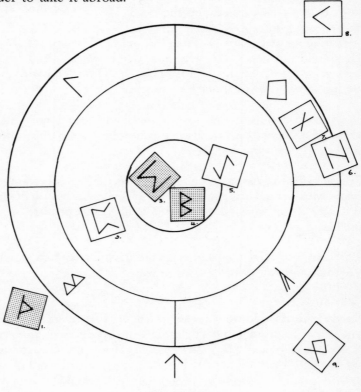

FIGURE 2

Major progression: Stones 1-5

1. Thorn hidden outside the circle: There is a danger that something vital to his immediate plans has been misunderstood and he must check this out.

2. Peorth outside Skjebne: It looks as if there are problems over assets or possessions he is trying to sell or dispose of. Once out of the way, things will go smoothly.

3. Eh in Skjebne: While there are problems to overcome the conclusion to his plans is in sight. All loose ends should be tied up.

4. Birca in Skjebne: Because his home is closely linked to his plans and, with it, his family, the scheme or future plan will further unify his family.

5. Yr in and outside Skjebne: This clearly says that the querent should avoid short cuts – rushing things in order to speed events. He should not make false economies and not overdo it.

Progression summary: This part of the cast clearly ties in with the querent's aims and ambitions. It warns the querent to make sure that every avenue has been explored in order to avoid delays, to do all necessary work properly as, in effect, he and his family will depend upon it.

Secondary progression: Stones 6 and 7

6. Hagal in Ing and outside circle: This clearly indicates events beyond the querent's control which will cause disruption.

7. Naut in Ing: This offers a warning to the querent to be prepared for problems and obstacles but to cope with them patiently and logically.

Progression summary: Outwardly not good news for the querent – the combination of these two stones reinforces the fact that difficulties will continue.

8. Single stone – Kaon outside the circle: The moves the querent intends will result in the loss of friends, and saying goodbye to people he knows. He must give this serious thought.

9. Single stone – Odal outside the circle: The querent must ensure that he is careful with any deals he undertakes. It could also point to machinery which is either unsafe or just unsound or unsuitable.

Cast summary
The cast clearly reveals that Geoffrey's intended venture will be a success although many frustrations before departure will cast doubts on the whole idea. He must also realize that he will be leaving many friends behind with, perhaps, the only benefit being a further unification of his family. He must prepare for his venture as best he can and not take short cuts. It indicates probable

mechanical problems and other difficulties prior to departure.

Result

At the time of writing Geoffrey has had considerable expenditure
on his craft. He discovered that it would not clear bridges on the
French canals and so the craft had to be ballasted to lower it in the
water. He has experienced numerous difficulties with items such
as generators and pumps. While the sale of remaining stock from
his business has been agreed, it has not been concluded.

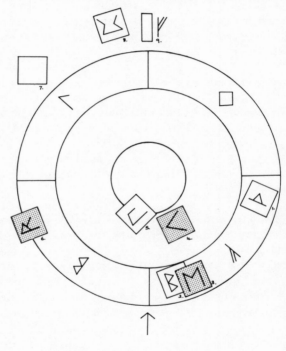

FIGURE 3

FIGURE 3

Name: Michael
Age: 36
Occupation: Reporter
Background: Recently divorced and now living with another
woman. His working situation is very insecure with a real chance
of impending redundancy.

1. Single stone – Thorn in Feoh: He can have what he most wants but it will be a question of biding his time and taking no undue risks. This stone points towards a major ambition or desire.

2 & 3. Group stones overlapping. Eh hidden on top of Birca both in Feoh: Here the combination of stones point towards a doomed marriage or partnership, but because this is closely linked to the existing family circle it might not necessarily involve the querent.

4. Single stone – Kaon hidden outside Skjebne: Regardless of the truth in the previous two stones, this single rune points towards the probability of the querent getting involved in an enjoyable yet unimportant affair.

5. Single stone – Ur in and out of Skjebne: In career terms, the querent must be ready to grasp a new opportunity from abroad. It will result in betterment, not possible in the present working situation. Delay in taking advantage of this opportunity could mean the loss of this chance – one which will not be repeated.

Stones 6 and 7 (not strictly a group but make better sense when read together):

6. Rit in Birca and outside the circle: The risks the querent has taken in his career or marriage will be his downfall and he will have to massively rethink his plans. This downturn will result in financial outlay for which he will have to make provision.

7. Skjebne outside the circle: The reversal of plans forecast in the previous rune were not just bad luck but a necessary lesson to be learned. The message here is clear: he must learn by his mistakes.

Group stones 8 and 9:

8. Peorth outside the circle: The querent must be prepared to be more content with his emotional lot, and not to look for 'that impossible dream'.

9. Feoh on edge outside the circle: This couples closely with rune eight pointing out that the querent has the chance to avoid further emotional upset, quarrels and clashes and possibly even separation, if he makes a positive effort with what he has. It could ge either

way – the result will be up to him.

Cast summary

This was an interesting cast in that the groups and single stones were not all observably connected. Here interpretations tended to dictate the logical groupings rather than the physical points the stones landed on. Clearly this cast warns the querent that all his ills are very much of his own making – there is no-one else to blame. Success, in both career and love, can be achieved if the querent gets his head out of the clouds and works hard in both areas. New opportunities will arise.

Result

Michael eventually lost his job but new opportunities arose – none from abroad but from elsewhere in the country. His new career is proving to be successful although his income is lower. His new family environment is a great success.

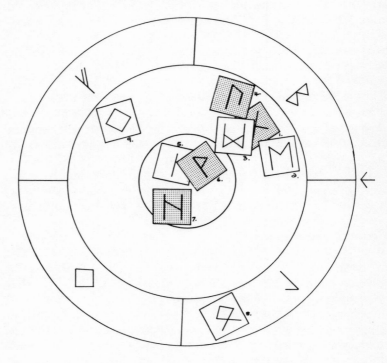

FIGURE 4

FIGURE 4

Name: Derek
Age: 53
Occupation: Representative
Background: Has been divorced for many years and has a girlfriend of many years standing. Lives alone and works as a freelance salesman.

Major group: Stones 1-4

1. Gifu hidden outside Skjebne: Someone, probably a woman, whom the querent has been close to and very fond of in the past is likely to return. This could result in him rethinking his current emotional status.

2. Eh outside Skjebne (resting on Gifu): This warns the querent that the 'lady from the past' must be viewed with caution. It could result in disruption and he must ask himself if his feelings are sincere or if it could be just a resurrected affair.

3. Man in and outside Skjebne (resting on Gifu): This is a complex situation for this rune with various interconnecting considerations. The stone points towards the querent's business activities but still affecting his overall lifestyle. The woman in stones one and two could also be involved. This stone warns the querent to 'beware of small print' or any details in a forthcoming contract. Treat any 'experimental' ideas with caution and simply pay attention to detail.

4. Ur hidden outside Skjebne (resting on Gifu): Again, this stone involves life's harmony, keeping things even and stable. An opportunity, unknown to the querent at the moment, will arise and could involve a change of home. This may not be for some time.

Group Summary: Clearly a warning is given to be careful when it comes to detail in business and thinking things through at an emotional level. Both could cause problems if not treated correctly. Further disruptions, but beneficial this time, are likely to come in the future.

5 & 6. Wunna hidden on top of Is in Skjebne: The querent is likely to leave the person he is truly fond of in the future and it will result in considerable sadness and the need for him to 'harden his heart'. Through Wunna it can be seen that a reunion will eventually take place under far better circumstances.

7. Single stone – Hagal in and slightly out of Skjebne: This stone indicates disruptions caused by natural events. The most obvious interpretation is that the querent is likely to suffer an illness in the future which could thwart or alter plans.

8. Single stone – Odal in Lagu: Personal goals for the querent will not be achieved the easy way; he must show will power and determination.

9. Single stone – Ing outside Skjebne: A clear pointer for the querent moving home to meet new faces and have new opportunities.

Cast summary
The querent should very much let his head rule his heart over business and emotional matters and pay attention to detail where both are concerned. New moves and a change of home are likely and while not achieved easily, will ultimately be successful.

Result
While the lady from the past has not yet reappeared, the querent has already lost business opportunities by not studying details or clearly communicating his wishes. At the moment plans are underway for the querent to move to a Mediterranean country within the next year and work is being geared to this end.

FIGURE 5

Name: Eileen
Age: 40
Occupation: Shopkeeper
Background: Having brought up her family alone for some years she is now established with a new man – someone who has his own clearly defined business interests, some of which overlap with those of her own. Considerable emotional upset preceded the new

established home arrangement. She is an astute businesswoman.

This cast shows six hidden stones and means that many unexpected events are likely to take place.

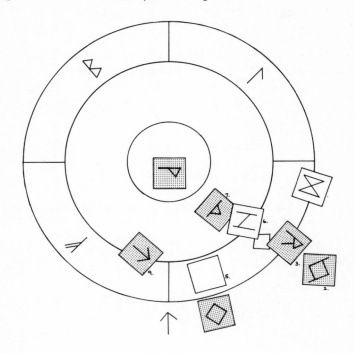

FIGURE 5

1. Single stone – Dag in Ing and outside the circle: Plans the querent is making and actively working towards will be more of a labour of love and will not be fully appreciated.

Group stones: 2 and 3 read together

2 & 3. Yer hidden outside the circle and Rit hidden in Ing: This warns the querent to try and keep her plans to herself for the time being. Also a subject which the querent is studying will prove to be a waste of time.

Group stones: 4 and 5 read together

4 & 5. Ing hidden outside the circle and Skjebne in Ing: Unknown

to the querent someone is likely to give a false account of something which affects her family and could result in a delicate situation which will have to be dealt with.

Group stones: 6 and 7 read together

6 & 7. Hagal outside Skjebne and in Ing resting on Thorn hidden outside Skjebne: Here again the querent will find herself in a situation not of her choosing and not to her advantage. In order to counter the stones' forecast, the querent must avoid hasty decisions.

8. Single stone – Wunna hidden in Skjebne: Someone close to the querent will return home unexpectedly – probably another woman. It will be an occasion for celebration.

9. Single stone – Tiu hidden in both Feoh and outside Skjebne: Something the querent has been secretly hoping for will soon happen. It could mean an extension of something which already exists – but on another 'wave-length'.

Cast summary
Part of the querent's time is spent on productive work but these activities will not be fully appreciated by someone else – maybe her new husband? It will, however, stand her in good stead for the future and have a bearing on new prospects both at home and work. Much of what happens will, apparently, be by 'accident' or out of her control. Stone eight is self-explanatory. Despite minor hiccups, the future looks assured.

Result
New business ventures are finally under way although this will mean a move of house. Her existing business has suffered following a reduction in passing trade caused by the opening of a new bypass nearby. She has taken up craft studies at a local college. Her eldest daughter recently returned home from South Africa. With the move of house comes the opportunity to involve herself in work in which she has always been interested.

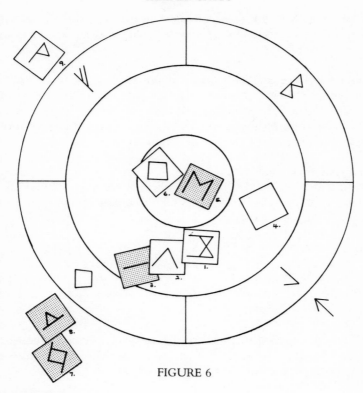

FIGURE 6

FIGURE 6

Name: Marjorie
Age: 51
Occupation: Theatrical Properties Manager
Background: Marjorie had an extremely unhappy childhood resulting from a broken home. She lives with an aged relative and her only leisure activity is boating. She has no emotional involvement – her last affair was with a well-known actor.

Major group: Stones 1-3

1. Man outside Skjebne: This indicates possible problems of a contractual nature and warns that misunderstandings are likely. The solution is to delegate nothing and act as her own messenger.

2. Kaon outside Skjebne: It follows that the misunderstanding will

be between her and someone she knows well – either a close friend or relative. Certainly the person in question is someone she much admires.

3. Is hidden in Lagu and outside Skjebne: Here some ambiguity comes in. It covers emotional cooling and it could refer to the querent seeing this friend or relative in a different light. But it could also refer to some asset being 'frozen', or tie in with the contractual problems already outlined.

Group summary
The querent is likely to lose something – possibly an asset or a friend – especially if she fails to attend to details and make herself clear in what she means.

Major progression: Stones 4-6

4. Skjebne outside Skjebne: The querent will soon be involved in a difficult situation which cannot remain unsolved and has been brewing for some time.

5. Eh hidden in Skjebne: Reforms, alterations, changes: these are impending. It will give the querent an opportunity to do what she wants to do for a change.

6. Ing in Skjebne and slightly in outside Skjebne: Changes or alterations to circumstances will be beneficial and will result in an entirely new phase in her life. It could indicate a change in home or living conditions.

Progression summary: All the stones so far point to a domestic rearrangement which will probably result in more freedom for the querent.

Group stones: 7 and 8 read together

7 & 8. Yer hidden in outside the circle and Thorn hidden outside the circle: This points again to poor communications and misunderstandings and warns that the querent should always make her intentions crystal clear. Some benefit the querent is waiting for or expecting will not happen and therefore plans must not be geared to this direction.

9. Single stone – Wunna outside the circle: While unattached at the moment the querent has deep affection for someone who she can see is doing everything wrong. She must take it upon herself to point that person in the right direction.

Cast summary
The querent should stop expecting that which will not happen and readjust her life accordingly. She will benefit from domestic changes. Her great weakness is in not making herself clearly understood and this could affect her forthcoming good fortune. She should have the courage to warn a close friend of his/her muddled thinking.

Result
Not a clear and concise cast and this probably reflects the way the querent is currently thinking (or not thinking!). None of the veiled benefits or changes in family circumstances have, at the time of writing, materialized.

Study of these six samples will show areas where ambiguities can crop up and it is in these situations that the diviner must carefully link the main themes, if not the primary meanings, of each stone in a group or progression. It is also an area where some intuitive application is needed.

It is interesting to observe, however, that those querents who treat the matter seriously and concentrate on what is at hand when they cast the stones, generally get the clearest, least ambiguous results. Is this a coincidence? Certainly the last querent in the six samples treated the whole matter with little regard and, as a result, the cast's results were, at best, trivial.

Before going any further, it would be a useful exercise for the budding practitioner to go through the samples shown here again and, without reference to interpretations offered, but using the meanings detailed in the following pages, produce his or her own set of results. Comparison between those published and your own will certainly indicate how satisfactorily you will be able to interpret your own runic casts.

6

FREYA'S EIGHT

FEOH ᚠ

This Rune governs *LOVE*.

Key words include: a feeling, kindness, tenderness, liking, affection, friendship, sentiment, longing, desire, romance, passion, hold dear, value, care for.

The Rune of FEOH (ᚠ) in SKJEBNE (▢)
Primary meaning: love that transcends the norm.
Subsidiary meanings: greater than usual, gigantic, vast, enormous, complete, collosal, breath taking, out of this world;
knows no bounds, soars, overwhelms, is superior to:
the normal, customary, standard pattern, model, the rule, formula, the usual, everyday.

The Rune of FEOH (ᚠ) outside SKJEBNE (◉)
Primary meaning: conserve to gain.
Subsidiary meanings: keep on ice, preserve, keep, protect, keep alive, store up, save up, build up a store, look after, cherish, treasure, maintain, service, feed;
in order to: win, profit, benefit, accumulate, earn, harvest, be rewarded, attain, reach, come into, win the jackpot, succeed.

The Rune of FEOH (ᚠ) in the Air quadrant (ᚠ)
Primary meaning: love hopes realized – contentment.
Subsidiary meanings: desires, longings, expectations, wants, needs, wishes for affection, tenderness, unity, passion;
converted into fact, given reality to, made to happen, come about, be done, exist;

bringing with them: pleasure, well-being, delight, happiness, pleased with one's lot, enjoyment.

The Rune of FEOH (⊬) in the Earth quadrant (⊳)
Primary meaning: well-being.
Subsidiary meanings: contentment, comfort, at ease, euphoria, peace, delight, happiness, agreeable, relish, feel pleasure, health and wealth, crest of the wave, success, good run of luck, golden touch, halcyon days, doing well, smile of fortune, bed of roses.

The Rune of FEOH (⊬) in the Water quadrant (◇)
Primary meaning: increase in love both physical and spiritual.
Subsidiary meanings: become greater, grow, enlarge, make bigger, tenderness, friendship, sentiment, longing, desire, romance, passion, hold dear, value, care for;
of the body, sensuous, natural, sexual; of the soul, mind, deep inner feelings, divine, inspired, almost sacred or religious.

The Rune of FEOH (⊬) in the Fire quadrant (⊦)
Primary meaning: marriage.
Subsidiary meanings: matrimony, wedlock, union, life together, conjugal bliss, love-match, nuptials, elope, man and wife, partners, good match, marry off, join, tie the knot, handfasting, pair off, for better for worse, set up house, repent at leisure.

The Rune of FEOH (⊬) outside the Runic circle (⊘)
Primary meaning: discord/divorce.
Subsidiary meanings: disagreement, controversy, argument, rows, bickering, clashes, rupture, breach, at odds, hostile, antagonistic, incompatible, quarrels, fighting, dissidence, loss of harmony;
go separate ways, break it up, cut loose, withdrawal, parting, be free, be alone, isolation, segregation, disconnect, untie the knot.

UR Π

This Rune governs *DISTANT INFLUENCES*.

Key words include: far away, remote in time or relation, not close or intimate, action invisibly exercised, exert upon, affect.

The Rune of UR (⋂) in SKJEBNE (▢)
Primary meaning: opportunities from afar – be ready to act.
Subsidiary meanings: possibilities, openings, well-timed, chances
to capitalize, twists of fate, scope, freedom, choices;
coming from: a distance, remote, out of range, ahead, back of
beyond, far away, not locally, at a distance, out of sight, at the
limit of vision.
Be prepared: alert, standing by, poised, forewarned, ready to go,
come into play, do, operate, try, move, have a go, perform,
participate.

The Rune of UR (⋂) outside SKJEBNE (◉)
Primary meaning: improvement through change.
Subsidiary meanings: betterment, an uplift, good influence, the
making of, enrichment, recovery, enhancement, increase,
restoration, rallying, turn the corner;
brought about by: alteration, variation, modification, adjustment,
contrast, variety, a break from routine, versatility, substitution of
one for another, ringing the changes, a shake-up.

The Rune of UR (⋂) in the Air quadrant (⼂)
Primary meaning: chance not to be wasted.
Subsidiary meanings: possibility, the right time, suitable opportunity, opening, heaven sent, stroke of luck, fortuitous, happy
accident, a gamble;
use it, exploit it, put to good use, must not be missed, get the best
out of it, turn it to account, profit by, avail yourself, capitalize,
cash in, take with both hands.

The Rune of UR (⋂) in the Earth quadrant (ß)
Primary meaning: think of tomorrow – do not be headstrong.
Subsidiary meanings: consider the future, study, meditate, worry
about, take into account, reflect, weigh up:
the day after today, prospects, the outlook, future, coming events,
what is to come, lies ahead, later, in due course, eventually,
ultimately.
Don't be: rash, reckless, impetuous, over-hasty, stubborn,
unyielding, perverse, obstinate, pig-headed, foolish.

The Rune of UR (⋂) in the Water quadrant (◇)
Primary meaning: visitors from afar.
Subsidiary meanings: people who: come, go to see, as an act of

friendship or social ceremony, on business, for curiosity, callers, drop in, come back, return, stay temporarily;
from far away, not locally, at a distance, other countries, continents, ways of life.

The Rune of UR (Π *) in the Fire quadrant (* Γ *)*
Primary meaning: have faith in your own judgement.
Subsidiary meanings: have: belief, credence, assurance, trust, accept, admit, swear by, go by, know, understand, rely on, have no doubt, depend on, hold:
your personal, not another's, independent, unaided, private opinion, sagacity, discernment, discretion, views, decisions, findings, rules, feelings, calculations, assessment.

The Rune of UR (Π *) outside the Runic circle (* ∅ *)*
Primary meaning: a chance wasted.
Subsidiary meanings: a possibility, the right time, suitable opportunity, opening, stroke of luck, happy accident, gamble:
gone forever, let slip, said goodbye to, irredeemable, misused, mishandled, not taken, spoiled, let go, missed, advantage not used.

THORN Þ

This rune governs *BENEFITS*.

Key words include: something to one's advantage, on one's behalf, in your own interest, for your own good, good turns, blessings.

The Rune of THORN (Þ *) in SKJEBNE (* ☐ *)*
Primary meaning: beneficial if you stay your hand.
Subsidiary meanings: it will be advantageous to: hold in abeyance, keep, reserve, hold over, delay, gain time, keep waiting, temporize, shelve, keep on ice – something which you are intending to do.
Don't: divulge, be too open, blurt out, spill the beans, come out with it, confide, confess, admit, let into the secret, tell what you are up to.

The Rune of THORN (▷) outside SKJEBNE (⬛)
Primary meaning: quick action leads to mistakes.
Subsidiary meanings: doing something at maximum speed, in a hurry, jumping in, at a gallop, in a short time, without reflection, break-neck, high speed, like a flash – will lead to:
errors, wrongness, faults, bad ideas, blunders, miscalculations, slips, being misled, being deceived, inaccuracy, clumsiness, being in the wrong, led up the garden path, playing into someone's hands.

The Rune of THORN (▷) in the Air quadrant (⼳)
Primary meaning: everything comes to he who waits.
Subsidiary meanings: if you: look on, wait and see, do nothing, be cautious, wary, heedful, discreet, take no risks, bide your time, leave nothing to chance – then, to you will come:
all things, all that matters, chances, rewards, credit, winnings, a rich harvest, you will collect, come in for, get the proceeds, inherit, things will fall to your share, come to you.

The Rune of THORN (▷) in the Earth quadrant (ᛒ)
Primary meaning: aggravating another will cause them to lash out; danger.
Subsidiary meanings: by exasperating, irritating, fanning the flames, complicating matters, making bad worse, you:
run the risk, skate on thin ice, tempt providence, court disaster, it's chancy, perilous; you will cause someone to:
erupt, be rude, violent, bellicose, run riot, rampage, see red, fume, explode, blow up, let fly, become maddened and angry.

The Rune of THORN (▷) in the Water quadrant (◇)
Primary meaning: not a time to gamble.
Subsidiary meanings: now is not the time to: take a risk, take the plunge, start a new venture, speculate, experiment, leap in the dark, play the market, hazard a try, chance it, try your luck.

The Rune of THORN (▷) in the Fire quadrant (ᚱ)
Primary meaning: do not let another manipulate you.
Subsidiary meanings: do not let someone else: pressure you, turn your head with honeyed words, goad you, crack the whip, motivate you with tempting offers and sales talk, work on you, call the tune, override your own feelings, shame you into something, manage you, set the pace, induce, persuade, win over.

The Rune of THORN (▷) outside the Runic Circle (⊘)
Primary meaning: misunderstandings – you did not make yourself clear.
Subsidiary meanings: because you were not: understandable, explicit, lucid, emphatic, did not use plain English and make things known – someone will: get the wrong end of the stick, be at cross purposes, misconstrue your meaning, twist the words, get a false reading.

OSS ᚠ

This Rune governs *INTERACTIONS*.

Key words include: acting reciprocally or on each other, give and take.

The Rune of OSS (ᚠ) in SKJEBNE (□)
Primary meaning: speedy decisions called for with an elderly person.
Subsidiary meanings: swift, fast, quick, lively, smart, expeditious, judgements, conclusions, decisions, settlements, evaluations, appraisals, summing up, taking stock –
will be necessary concerned with someone – of pensionable age, of declining years, with grey hairs, in their dotage, second childhood, senile, old, wrinkled, doddering, past it.

The Rune of OSS (ᚠ) outside SKJEBNE (◉)
Primary meaning: gain in knowledge that leads to an important action.
Subsidiary meanings: acquiring, getting, increasing, attaining more: comprehension, cognition, understanding, grasp, mastery, wisdom, learning, experience, know how –
this will lead to a: serious, grave, urgent, vital, supreme, weighty, solemn, critical, fateful, no joke, life and death –
gesture, conduct, occurrence, step, tactic, manoeuvre, measure, move, behaviour, deal, transaction, attempt, commitment.

The Rune of OSS (ᚠ) in the Air quadrant (⊬)
Primary meaning: love to cross the age barrier.
Subsidiary meanings: affection, friendship, sentiment, fondness, longing, lust, desire, harmony, closeness, appeal, charm, fascination, attraction;

between two people years apart, a young lover, father figure, mother substitute, sugar daddy – people with similar interests but from different age groups.

The Rune of OSS (ᚠ) in the Earth quadrant (ᛒ)
Primary meaning: long life.
Subsidiary meanings: longevity, ripe old age, long duration, long innings, into extra time, outlive others, wear well, endure, last, survive, evergreen, long run.

The Rune of OSS (ᚠ) in the Water quadrant (◇)
Primary meaning: partnership improved by quick action.
Subsidiary meanings: a joint effort: duet, team work, mutual assistance, give and take, relationship, marriage, unity, think alike, inseparable, hand in hand, work together, pull together; will be made better: built up, stronger, developed, increased, gain, advance, amplified, enhanced;
by: speedy, swift, fast, lively, smart, expeditious, gestures, conduct, steps, tactics, manoeuvres, measures, behaviour, moves, deals, transactions, attempts, commitments.

The Rune of OSS (ᚠ) in the Fire quadrant (ᚱ)
Primary meaning: an older person's advice benefits partnership.
Subsidiary meanings: an opinion given as to future action – counsel, information, knowledge, hints, suggestions, warnings: Received from: someone advanced in age, not young, with experience, older and wiser, long established, mature, of another age;
will: do good, help, make better, enhance a relationship, marriage, joint effort, team work, unity.

The Rune of OSS (ᚠ) outside the Runic circle (⊘)
Primary meaning: do not delegate. Be careful – small accident.
Subsidiary meanings: do not: deputize, act for, on behalf of, appear for, negotiate or stand in for, replace, do duty of, substitute, hold the baby, pass the buck.
Be warned: take heed, caution, pay attention, on guard, forewarned, painstaking, watchful.
Not large, little, paltry, trifling, silly, slight error, unexpected event, chance mishap, unintentional act, fluke, unpredictable event.

RIT ᚱ

This rune governs *CAREER*.

Key words include: trade, profession, calling, life-work, bread and butter, craft, job, employment, occupation, calling, chosen work.

The Rune of RIT (ᚱ) in SKJEBNE (◻)
Primary meaning: success where most deserved.
Subsidiary meanings: happy ending, accomplishment, achievement, victory, win, attainment of object, reach goal, triumph, make out, come off well, conquer, breakthrough;
where most: merited, earned, due, owing, credited, expected, warranted, valid, worked hard for.

The Rune of RIT (ᚱ) outside SKJEBNE (▣)
Primary meaning: through own effort there is success. You go far – travel.
Subsidiary meanings: because of, by, by way of: personal, private, individual, not aided by anyone else –
steps taken, doing, performance, labour, stress, trouble, hard work, will power, exertion –
there will be: happy ending, accomplishment, achievement, victory, winning, attainment of object, reach goal, triumph, break through. You will also: journey, visit other countries, see the world, move from place to place.

The Rune of RIT (ᚱ) in the Air quadrant (ᚠ)
Primary meaning: a love adventure.
Subsidiary meanings: office romance, love affair, flirtation, amour, entanglement, intrigue, lover, admirer, infatuation, passing ships, something that takes your fancy, light relief, escapade.

The Rune of RIT (ᚱ) in the Earth quadrant (ᛒ)
Primary meaning: risk, be prepared, unexpected expenses.
Subsidiary meanings: element of uncertainty, not one hundred per cent sure, gamble, chance, peril, dangers, hazards;
be warned, ready, take care, precautions, tread carefully, be alert, keep your eyes open;
unforseen, unknown, not bargained for, taken aback, surprise, out of the blue, jolt, a start;

expenditure, outlay, costs, outgoings, not budgeted for, out of pocket.

The Rune of RIT (ᛉ) in the Water quadrant (◇)
Primary meaning: hold back knowledge, do not reveal your hand.
Subsidiary meanings: keep back what you know, have learned, are aware of, informed about;
don't disclose, communicate, leak, give away, confess, let on, indicate, admit, expose, show, confide, betray, come out with – what you are up to, keep your plans secret, keep things to yourself, don't be too open, play it close to your chest.

The Rune of RIT (ᛉ) in the Fire quadrant (ᚱ)
Primary meaning: much patience needed.
Subsidiary meanings: what is required – good temper, calmness, imperturbability, steadiness, composure, coolness, forebearance, endurance, long-suffering, longanimity, tolerance, toleration, sufferance, resignation, acquiescence, submission, keep calm, master your feelings, put up with it, grin and bear it.

The Rune of RIT (ᛉ) outside the Runic circle (∅)
Primary meaning: an upset of plans.
Subsidiary meanings: inversion, turning back to front, inside out, overturning, change, turnabout, shuffle, otherway round, reversal, spoiling, messed up:
intentions, calculations, purpose, decisions, designs, schemes, plots, pursuits, aims, course of action, desired object, resolves, aspirations, targets, dreams, desires.

KAON ᚲ

This Rune governs *RELATIONSHIPS*.

Key words include: involvements, concerns, rapport, bonds, links, relativity, comparisons, friendships, ties with, bearings upon.

The Rune of KAON (ᚲ) in SKJEBNE (◻)
Primary meaning: someone from your past to return.
Subsidiary meanings: a person you once knew, an old school friend, colleague, lover, friend, acquaintance, known to you before;

come back, re-enter, make an appearance, crop up, recur,
reappear, afresh, now, echo of the past.

The Rune of KAON (<) outside SKJEBNE (⬒)
Primary meaning: a light relationship.
Subsidiary meanings: love affair, flirtation, entanglement, intrigue,
lover, admirer, amorous adventure, infatuation, passing ships,
light relief.

The Rune of KAON (<) in the Air quadrant (Ⱶ)
Primary meaning: for a lady, a gift; for a man, the joy of giving.
Subsidiary meanings: a present, treat, surprise, unexpected
present, little thank you, chocolates, an expression of love or
thanks;
Pleasure in giving, thing that causes delight, emotion of pleasure,
better to give than to receive.

The Rune of KAON (<) in the Earth quadrant (ß)
Primary meaning: improvement leading to revitalization.
Subsidiary meanings: betterment, uplift, amelioration, change
for the better, transfiguration, conversion, enrichment, enchance-
ment, upswing;
leading to new strength, fresh energies, resuscitate, regenerate,
resurrect, freshen, rekindle, rejuvenate, revive, pick up, come to
life again.

The Rune of KAON (<) in the Water quadrant (◇)
Primary meaning: an opportunity or a relationship which must be
acted upon.
Subsidiary meanings: a chance, access, well-timed possibility,
opening, scope, choice;
or an involvement, friendship, link, bond, concern, which must
be: followed up, not ignored, put into operation, worked on,
brought into play, handled, manipulated, taken advantage of,
seized.

The Rune of KAON (<) in the Fire quadrant (Γ)
Primary meaning: much to be gained by encouraging.
Subsidiary meanings: a great deal, a large amount, something
vast:
to be acquired, learned, got, won, earned, obtained, piled up, got
hold of, increase, expansion, profit by, get rich, gain by inspiring,

approval, egg on, allow or promote continuance or progress of, inspire with courage, embolden, stimulate by assistance.

The Rune of KAON (< *) outside the Runic circle (* ∅ *)*
Primary meaning: loss of a friendship through a silly mistake.
Subsidiary meanings: be deprived of, forfeit, waste, sacrifice, privation, missing, said goodbye to:
a friend, relationship, closeness, amity, concord, fellowship, compatibility, warmth, kindness;
because of, by way of, caused by: an absurd, foolish, stupid, ridiculous, trifling error, slip, bad idea, fault, misunderstanding.

GIFU ✕

This Rune governs *BALANCE*.

Key words include: equilibrium, even-sided, correspondence, equality, parallel, harmony, rhythm, even, both sides equal.

The Rune of GIFU (✕ *) in SKJEBNE (* ◻ *)*
Primary meaning: a coming together brings rich rewards.
Subsidiary meanings: an assemblage, gathering, rally, meeting, celebration, social group, reunion, crowd, put together, join, attract, unite;
causes, results in, brings about, conveys,
great compensation, gratitude, high fees, great honours, much acclaim, generosity, tributes, presents, hearty thanks.

The Rune of GIFU (✕ *) outside SKJEBNE (* ◉ *)*
Primary meaning: reunion in the near future.
Subsidiary meanings: harmony, unison, agreement, see eye to eye, come together again, not be parted, reunite, join together, be one again, reconciliation, another try.

The Rune of GIFU (✕ *) in the Air quadrant (* ⴹ *)*
Primary meaning: not a time to stand alone.
Subsidiary meanings: circumstances warn against, no apt, not right, now now, don't, take note, be warned, omens are not right, the wrong moment –
to: go it alone, stick your neck out, attempt by yourself, seek help, advice, counsel, someone or other people to assist you, get some

backing, someone behind you, don't take it all on your own shoulders.

The Rune of GIFU (✕) in the Earth quadrant (ᛒ)
Primary meaning: more give than take needed.
Subsidiary meanings: a greater degree of, an increase in, additional devotion, dedication, concessions, allowances, impart more, relax, yield to pressure, elasticity, presents;
not so much: seizing, obtaining, exacting, using, capturing – is is required, called for, necessary, demanded, wanted, what must be done.

The Rune of GIFU (✕) in the Water quadrant (◇)
Primary meaning: seek advice.
Subsidiary meanings: look for, search, find, ask for, hunt, quest for:
counsel, words of wisdom, criticism, tips, hints, reference, consult, suggestions, recommendations, refer, confide in, listen to, be advised, submit one's judgement to another's, put heads together, compare notes, sit in conclave, ask for opinions.

The Rune of GIFU (✕) in the Fire quadrant (ᚦ)
Primary meaning: success linked to another.
Subsidiary meanings: attainment of object, favourable issue, happy ending, time well spent, take the prize, triumph, gain, glory, victory;
connected with, joined, caused, in conjunction with:
someone else, additional, different, similar, some other person, a second party.

The Rune of GIFU (✕) outside the Runic circle (⊘)
Primary meaning: a quarrel.
Subsidiary meanings: bickering, friction, fall out, severance of friendly relations, at odds, aggression, feud, tiff, squabble, occasion for complaint, have differences, at loggerheads, nag, spoiling for a fight, bellicose, dispute with, cat and dog, row.

WUNNA ᚹ

This Rune governs *EARTHLY LOVE.*

Key words include: terrestrial, of or on the earth, not a spiritual or higher affection, friendship, fondness, closeness, passion, desire, physical attraction, bodily.

The Rune of WUNNA (▷) in SKJEBNE (▢)
Primary meaning: a loved one returns – celebrations.
Subsidiary meanings: a close friend, member of the family, old flame, someone who is loved and has been parted from you – comes back, comes home, arrives, drops in, turns up, puts in an appearance, returns to the nest.
This causes cheerfulness, happiness, mirth, jollity, occasions for rejoicing, merry-making, parties, family get-togethers.

The Rune of WUNNA (▷) outside SKJEBNE (▣)
Primary meaning: good news connected with a loved one.
Subsidiary meanings: pleasing, beneficial, first rate, most desirable, excellent, couldn't be better – information, communication, letter, phone call, results;
concerned with: a close friend, member of the family, husband, wife.

The Rune of WUNNA (▷) in the Air quadrant (Ⲏ)
Primary meaning: prospects are golden.
Subsidiary meanings: the future outlook, coming events, what is to come, in the fullness of time, in due course,
show very good signs, have the makings of, show promise, good omens, of turning out: balmy, halcyon, favourable, auspicious, doing well, smile of fortune, Midas touch, blessed, couldn't be better.

The Rune of WUNNA (▷) in the Earth quadrant (ꛛ)
Primary meaning: take what the future offers.
Subsidiary meanings: convert to use, enjoy what's at your disposal, exploit, use, avail yourself, employ, make use of, use to the full, take up;
what is to come, in the offing, in view, about to be, on the point of, imminent; turns up, provided, furnished, given, supplied, produced, yielded.

The Rune of WUNNA (▷) in the Water quadrant (◇)
Primary meaning: gain from giving to a loved one.
Subsidiary meanings: a chance to: increase, get, win, acquire, reap,

profit, earn a dividend, succeed,
by: bestowing generosity, gifts, presents, something extra, token,
labour of love, offering, sacrifice, contribute, hand over;
to someone close: a friend, relative, husband, wife, sweetheart.

The Rune of WUNNA (ᚹ *) in the Fire quadrant (* ᚱ *)*
Primary meaning: open your heart to a loved one.
Subsidiary meanings: uncover, lay bare, expose, unveil, show,
keep nothing back or hidden –
affections, feelings, passions, emotions, mental and spiritual
make-up, soul, inner self, sentiments, responses, eagerness,
deeply felt, sincere, be demonstrative, don't hide your feelings –
to someone close: a friend, relative, husband, wife, sweetheart.

The Rune of WUNNA (ᚹ *) outside the Runic circle (* ⊘ *)*
Primary meaning: risks around a loved one.
Subsidiary meanings: chance of bad consequences, perils, dangers,
pitfalls, traps, threats, warnings, danger signals, evil omens,
chancy dangerous courses;
on every side, all about, surrounding, encompassing, enclosing,
ringing round, closing in;
around: a close friend, relative, husband, wife, sweetheart.

7

HAGAL'S EIGHT

HAGAL ᚺ

This Rune governs *DISRUPTIONS*.

Key words include: upheavals, splits, separations, shambles, scenes of chaos, violent dissolutions.

The Rune of HAGAL (ᚺ *) in SKJEBNE (* □ *)*
Primary meaning: disruptions caused by nature.
Subsidiary meanings: scenes of chaos, upheavals, splits, separations, havoc, plans wrecked, hopes suffocated,
all brought about by natural forces: floods, fire, earthquake, lightning, death, illness, acts of God.

The Rune of HAGAL (ᚺ *) in any other position on the Runic Chart*
Primary meaning: events beyond your control.
Subsidiary meanings: it is: out of your power, influence, cannot be manipulated, there are no strings to pull, you have no sway, no say in or authority over:
happenings, occurrences, opportunities, mishaps, emergencies, the state of affairs, current happenings and concerns, what is on the agenda, arises, in the wind, falls to one's lot.

NAUT ᚼ

This rune governs *WARNINGS*.

Key words include: danger signals, omens, writing on the wall, predictions, forecasts, prophecies.

The Rune of NAUT (┤) in SKJEBNE (☐)
Primary meaning: warning: care and constraint.
Subsidiary meanings: this is a danger signal: be cautious, look out, keep watch, take notice, be on your guard.
You must be prepared to: take pains, give attention to detail, take heed, be thorough, exact, feel your way.
Also required are: temperance, restriction, self-control, keep things on a lead, under control, within bounds, confined, with strings attached.

The Rune of NAUT (┤) outside SKJEBNE (▣)
Primary meaning: patience.
Subsidiary meanings: the following qualities may be called for: be resolute, single-minded, have staying power, be steady, unflagging, undaunted, never despair, you must have what it takes to continue, stick to it, keep at it, be good-tempered, calm, tolerant, enduring, forebearing, resigned and prepared to put up with matters.

The Rune of NAUT (┤) in the Air quadrant (ⱀ)
Primary meaning: perseverence.
Subsidiary meanings: the following qualities may be called for: persistence, tenacity, stubbornness, single-mindedness, concentration, plodding on, staying power, grit, be a willing horse, unfailing, never discouraged, keep at it, never say die, stick to your guns.

The Rune of NAUT (┤) in the Earth quadrant (ß)
Primary meaning: rash acts hold back plans.
Subsidiary meanings: by being incautious, heedless, inconsiderate, flippant, over-confident, dare-devil, irresponsible, frivolous, playing with fire, having a couldn't-care-less attitude; this sort of conduct, behaviour, exploits will only serve to:
retard future intentions and ambitions, delay the reaching of goals and targets as well as aims, hopes and calculations.

The Rune of NAUT (┤) in the Water quadrant (◇)
Primary meaning: stumbling blocks.
Subsidiary meanings: the following all have a certain nuisance value and can get in the way or hinder progress: impediments, obstructions, frustrations, checks, snags, a spot of trouble, interference, hurdles, blind alleys, brick walls, handicaps,

meddling, sabotage, teething troubles, problems.

The Rune of NAUT (✦) in the Fire quadrant (⌐)
Primary meaning: refusals.
Subsidiary meanings: non-acceptance, a shake of the head, saying no, a slap in the face, unwillingness, something withheld, being turned down, declining an offer, turning a deaf ear to suggestions, frowned upon, refusal of consent, not wanted.

The Rune of NAUT (✦) outside the Runic Circle (⌀)
Primary meaning: gossip.
Subsidiary meanings: something to tell, tit-bits, causing a sensation, unconfirmed reports, hearsay, talk of the town, tittle-tattle, scandal-mongers, the inside story, common knowledge, indiscretions, nudges and winks, interference, side glances, whispering, talking behind someone's back.

IS |

This Rune governs *EMOTIONAL COOLING.*

Key words include: indifference, loss of interest, lukewarm feelings, half-hearted, unresponsive, no enthusiasm, no passion, no longer eager, no longer deeply felt.

The Rune of IS (|) in SKJEBNE (☐)
Primary meaning: spiritual pain caused by partings.
Subsidiary meanings: in the soul, heart, mind, breast, bottom of one's heart, deep-felt, sincere feelings of:
distress, strain, hurt, ache, torment, prolonged agony, wretchedness, bruised, miserable, sadness, having a thin time, brought about by: separation, a break-up, someone gone away, divorce, being kept apart, disunion, a wedge between you.

The Rune of IS (|) outside SKJEBNE (▣)
Primary meaning: cooling of emotions.
Subsidiary meanings: feelings of indifference, disinterest, half-hearted, lukewarm, unresponsive, no enthusiasm, no passion, no longer eager, no deep feelings, go off someone, see the person for what they are.

The Rune of IS (|) in the Air quadrant (Ƴ)
Primary meaning: one-sided love.
Subsidiary meanings: uneven, by one party only, friendship, affection, tenderness and fondness which is not shared, love-hate, infatuation, a crush, calf-love, an idol, heart-throb, only out for what they can get, being used.

The Rune of IS (|) in the Earth quadrant (ß)
Primary meaning: broken hearts.
Subsidiary meanings: melancholy, heart-broken, sorrowful, woebegone, unhappy, tormented, wretched, misery, tears, anguish, regretful, feeling ill-used, taking things badly.

The Rune of IS (|) in the Water quadrant (◇)
Primary meaning: frozen assets.
Subsidiary meanings: matters are being kept on ice, suspended, preserved, kept alive but cooled, reserves and resources are frozen until needed.

The Rune of IS (|) in the Fire quadrant (⌐)
Primary meaning: static.
Subsidiary meanings: immobile, at rest, still, asleep, stagnating, at a standstill, unmoving, stuck, riding at anchor, staying put, lying low, keeping quiet.

The Rune of IS (|) outside the Runic circle (⊘)
Primary meaning: divorce – separation.
Subsidiary meanings: disconnect, withdrawal, parting of the ways, isolation, segregation, break-up, cut loose, break away, unclasp, detach, go separate ways, be alone, avoid each other, be free.

YER ◇

This Rune governs *LESSONS*.

Key words include: examples, cautions, warnings, profit by example, what must be learned, take heed, learning, self improvement, study, gain knowledge.

The Rune of YER (⋄) in SKJEBNE (▢)
Primary meaning: a waiting period.
Subsidiary meanings: passivity, dormancy, nothing-doing, stagnation, doldrums, inactivity, in abeyance, lying fallow, inert, wait and see, look on, procrastinate, unemployed, unprogressive, idle, slack water.

The Rune of YER (⋄) outside SKJEBNE (▣)
Primary meaning: static.
Subsidiary meanings: stagnation, asleep, immobile, rest, stillness, at a standstill, unmoving, stuck, stay put, ride at anchor, keep quiet, unruffled, poker-faced.

The Rune of YER (⋄) in the Air quadrant (Ⱶ)
Primary meaning: legal documents – you gain after waiting.
Subsidiary meanings: official, required or appointed by law, based on or within the province of the law;
written papers, manuscripts, contracts, deeds, treaties, writs, warrants;
you will: acquire, profit, succeed, come by, increase, later, subsequently, following;
bide time, be patient, hold on, abstain from action, pause, tarry, keep watch.

The Rune of YER (⋄) in the Earth quadrant (ᛒ)
Primary meaning: slow up – regain energy.
Subsidiary meanings: decelerate, don't overdo things, don't take on too much, ease up, put on the brakes, shorten sail, reduce speed, rein in, check, curb, back pedal;
give yourself a chance to: revive, pick up, recharge your batteries, rally, come round, recover, get well, recuperate, return to normal, become yourself again.

The Rune of YER (⋄) in the Water quadrant (◇)
Primary meaning: look to the long-term – safeguard yourself legally.
Subsidiary meanings: watch out for, be aware of, have regard for, attend to, take notice of, keep an eye on, remember;
long duration, future, permanence, long standing, security, not now but in years to come, future generations, the remainder;
make provision, stipulations, precautions, protect, officially, binding, based on or within the province of the law.

The Rune of YER ($\Diamond$) in the Fire quadrant (r)
Primary meaning: look closely to detail.
Subsidiary meanings: pay attention, take notice, have regard, attend to, take heed, keep an eye on, take pains, concentrate, have a care, watch out;
seemingly insignificant matters, be exact, precise, be thorough, right to the last detail, careful, diligent, meticulous, check and re-check, an eye to detail, exact, minute.

The Rune of YER ($\Diamond$) outside the Runic circle ($\varnothing$)
Primary meaning: you wait in vain.
Subsidiary meaning: you are patient, hold on, defer action with a view to something expected, bide time, keep watch, do nothing, don't make a decision –
to no purpose, without success, empty, doomed to failure, without regard, achieve nothing, to no avail.

YR $\int$

This Rune governs *OUTWARD JOURNEYS*.

Key words include: directed towards the external, material, visible, apparent, travels, expeditions, quests, searches.

The Rune of YR ($\int$) in SKJEBNE ($\Box$)
Primary meaning: trouble averted by going the long way round.
Subsidiary meanings: bother, inconvenience, exertion, vexation, grief, pains, the thing which causes this, anxiety;
turned away, warded off, missed,
by taking not the shortest, far-reaching, no short-cuts, method, procedure, course, manner, form, means, channel, road, technique, course of action.

The Rune of YR ($\int$) outside SKJEBNE ($\boxdot$)
Primary meaning: success if you don't overdo things.
Subsidiary meanings: attainment of object, favourable issue, happy ending, time well spent, triumph, glory, victory,
if you don't: go to extremes, overtire yourself, take on too much, strain yourself, bite off more than you can chew, exaggerate, over-act, aggravate, over-emphasize, make too important, enlarge, magnify, make mountains out of molehills.

The Rune of YR (ʃ) in the Air quadrant (Ⲩ)
Primary meaning: don't over-react.
Subsidiary meanings: don't exaggerate your emotions or feelings, don't go into hysterics at the slightest little thing, keep cool, don't get flustered or heated by events, don't make too much out of a situation.

The Rune of YR (ʃ) in the Earth quadrant (ß)
Primary meaning: pause.
Subsidiary meanings: calm down, cool off, unwind a little, don't go dashing about wildly, sit back and take stock, ease up, take some time off, cool your vibes, don't get so angry, worried, involved, upset, take a deep breath before starting again.

The Rune of YR (ʃ) in the Water quadrant (◇)
Primary meaning: look calm when flustered.
Subsidiary meanings: look still, serene, unruffled, unabashed, undisturbed, not in the least bit bothered or worried –
when inside you are: confused, in a flurry, nervous, at sixes and sevens, agitated, in a bustle, panicking, don't quite know what to do but must do something.

The Rune of YR (ʃ) in the Fire quadrant (⌐)
Primary meaning: irksome problems.
Subsidiary meanings: tedious, tiresome, boring, wearisome, same, repetitious, no fun, uninteresting, unamusing, try your patience, monotonous, unvarying;
difficulties, perplexities, enigmas, burdens, troubles, tasks, jobs, predicaments, tough assignments, things to be sorted out, coped with.

The Rune of YR (ʃ) outside the Runic circle (⊘)
Primary meaning: overtired, strain, the rope snaps.
Subsidiary meanings: made excessive demands on person's strength, damaged by exertion, weary through toil, labour, over-taxed, exhausted, on your knees;
tension, distorted from body stress, stretched beyond normal degree, sudden breakdown, fracture, collapse, sudden giving way, failure, stop of mental energy, sudden loss of courage and spirits.

PEORTH ⊠

This Rune governs *SEXUALITY*.

Key words include: of sex, occurring between the two sexes, desires, passions, animal instincts, urges.

The Rune of PEORTH (⊠) in SKJEBNE (▢)
Primary meaning: keep the secret.
Subsidiary meanings: secrecy, silence, mystery, keep it dark, keep close, under your hat, mum, reserve, withhold, let it go no further, be taciturn, to yourself, tell no-one, don't breathe a word, lock up, bottle up, conceal, protect, guard, hide, lock in, never tell.

The Rune of PEORTH (⊠) outside SKJEBNE (▣)
Primary meaning: material gain.
Subsidiary meanings: concerned with bodily comforts, things, assets, possessions, worldly not spiritual, money, belongings, goods and chattels;
acquisition, getting, winning, earning, obtaining, build up a store, get hold of, come by, increase, expand, profit, grow rich.

The Rune of PEORTH (⊠) in the Air quadrant (Ⱶ)
Primary meaning: a gift.
Subsidiary meanings: a natural flair, inborn ability, aptitude, knack, genius for, present, token, reward, consideration, prize, something extra, free of cost, given away, had for the asking, windfall, acquisition, come by.

The Rune of PEORTH (⊠) in the Earth quadrant (ᛒ)
Primary meaning: be on your guard – sexual health hazard.
Subsidiary meanings: be warned, take care, precautions, be alert, watch out, careful;
something damaging or injurious to health, well-being, constitution, brought about sexually: unwanted pregnancy, V.D. – who knows? you are warned.

The Rune of PEORTH (⊠) in the Water quadrant (◇)
Primary meaning: take no chances – all is not what it seems.
Subsidiary meanings: take no risks, make certain, calculate the odds, do nothing casually, unintentionally, on the spur of the

moment, whatever happens make sure, avoid doing anything hasty;
appearances are misleading, deceptive, it is not as good as it may appear, misguiding, unreal, a delusion, contradiction, sham, make-believe, imitation, farce, concealed.

The Rune of PEORTH (ᛩ) in the Fire quadrant (ᚱ)
Primary meaning: reveal nothing.
Subsidiary meanings: disclose, communicate, leak, give away, confess, let on, indicate, admit, expose, show, unveil, blurt out, spill, come clean, confide, come out with, betray, report; tell nobody, not a soul, don't say a word, blank, nought, zero, hold back, don't reveal anything.

The rune of PEORTH (ᛩ) outside the Runic circle (∅)
Primary meaning: be more realistic or you will be disappointed.
Subsidiary meanings: get matters in their proper perspective, sorted out, don't expect or hope for too much, what is not possible, get your feet on the ground, face up to things, see it as it actually is, what is genuine, not artificial –
or you will: feel let down, disenchanted, disillusioned, made unhappy, desires and expectations not fulfilled.

AQUIZI ᛣ

This Rune governs *THE HIGHER LAW, THE SOUL.*

Key words include: spirit, heart, mind, the inner you.

The Rune of AQUIZI (ᛣ) in SKJEBNE (☐)
Primary meaning: circle out more.
Subsidiary meanings: find new company, ideas, past-times, try something new, make new friends, broaden your horizons, widen your knowledge, stretch yourself, branch out, let yourself go, seek new interests and circles to move in.

The Rune of AQUIZI (ᛣ) outside SKJEBNE (▣)
Primary meaning: new career, changes in work and home.
Subsidiary meanings: a change of job, activity, occupation, employment, duties, what one has to do, their field, department, line of country;

alterations, a shift of scene, pastures new, a turning point both at home and work.

The Rune of AQUIZI (Y) in the Air quadrant (⊬)
Primary meaning: decision about long-term future – do not hold back.
Subsidiary meanings: a time to judge facts, recapitulate, inspect, assess, consider, form an opinion, do a survey, find solutions which will affect:
what is to come, your destiny, what's on the agenda for a long time to come, something permanent, deep-rooted, lasting.
Don't be tempted to keep quiet about something which bothers you, bottle things up, curb your feelings; if you want to express an opinion or an idea, now is the time to do so.

The Rune of AQUIZI (Y) in the Earth quadrant (⌐)
Primary meaning: don't be used; spiritual vampires drain.
Subsidiary meanings: don't be: exploited, taken in, duped, manipulated, utilized;
don't allow others to: prey on, become parasites, wring out, dry up, soak up, absorb, dehydrate, reduce your:
unconscious, personality, ego, mind, heart, soul.

The Rune of AQUIZI (Y) in Water quadrant (◇)
Primary meaning: study (hidden factors); expansion, strength from outside.
Subsidiary meanings: be careful, surveillant, attentive, take notice, be aware, look out, pay attention, be alert;
opportunities for increase, enlargement, amplification, reflation, growth, flowering out, deepening, heightening, building up, development, making more mighty and potent will be found externally, lie beyond.

The Rune of AQUIZI (Y) in the Fire quadrant (Γ)
Primary meaning: give more of yourself, the all-embracing nature.
Subsidiary meanings: make your identity known, don't hold back, come out of your shell, show your personality, be outgoing, put in more effort, be wholehearted, body and soul, one hundred per cent, every inch, no omissions, totally, entirely, undivided attention.

The Rune of AQUIZI (Y *) outside the Runic circle (* ∅ *)*
Primary meaning: serendipity – happy accident.
Subsidiary meanings: accidental discovery, finding, treasure
trove, hit upon, no assignable cause, fortuitous, turn of fate, fall to
one's lot, chance upon, unaccountable, lucky shot;
brings pleasure, enjoyment, a pleasant time, good luck, will
delight, be appreciated.

SIG ⌇

This Rune governs *DECISIONS*.

Key words include: chose, calculate, conclude, deduce, appraise,
consider, pass judgement, sum up, make up mind, course of
action.

The Rune of SIG (⌇ *) in SKJEBNE (* □ *)*
Primary meaning: wait – answers found through time.
Subsidiary meanings: wait and see, mark time, while away, do
nothing for the time being, tread water, hang fire, delay, be
inactive, don't decide yet, suspend operations –
because: explanations, reasons, light, clarification, solutions,
keys, clues, illustrations, courses –
will be found: in due course, in the future, in a while, later, to
come, lie ahead, yet to come, not now, another day.

The Rune of SIG (⌇ *) outside SKJEBNE (* ◎ *)*
Primary meaning: you try what is beyond you.
Subsidiary meanings: you attempt, strive after, tackle, endeavour,
search, struggle for, venture, undertake, take on, devote yourself,
gamble, quest, take on obligations –
which are: outside your range, scope, capabilities, not possible,
too much, hopeless, no chance, impracticable, out of the
question, unfeasible, unworkable, unachievable.

The Rune of SIG (⌇ *) in the Air quadrant (* ¥ *)*
Primary meaning: stop now and regain energy.
Subsidiary meanings: now is the time to halt, desist, refrain, down
tools, switch off, relax, rest, finish, break off, withdraw;
give yourself a chance to revive, pick up, rally, come round,
recover, recharge your batteries, get well, recuperate, return to

normal, sleep it off, become yourself again.

The Rune of SIG (⚡) in the Earth quadrant (ᛒ)
Primary meaning: worry – negative feelings, concentrate, mind over matter.
Subsidiary meanings: there are feelings of uneasiness, disquiet, cares, problems, headaches, anxiety, woe, bad feelings generally, undercurrents, pulses, tremors;
you must think, collect your thoughts, be attentive, consider, contemplate, reflect, get it together,
and also: use your brain, intelligence, perception to sort things out, not physical strength.

The Rune of SIG (⚡) in the Water quadrant (◇)
Primary meaning: necessary expenditure will lead to gain.
Subsidiary meanings: force of circumstances will dictate, impose, require, give no choice, be unforgoable, bring about unavoidable, outgoings: costs, expenses, outlay, investment, disbursements, spending, out of pocket expenditure;
but this will lead to: profit, gain, winnings, acquisition, success, earning a dividend, making money, reap rewards, a rich harvest.

The Rune of SIG (⚡) in the Fire quadrant (ᚱ)
Primary meaning: stay calm and stay put.
Subsidiary meanings: it is necessary to remain imperturbable, steady, composed, cool, serene, tranquil, content, unexcitable, unworried, good-tempered, relaxed.
It is also necessary to be inert, stand firm, mark time, quiesce, sit tight, ride at anchor, don't move, be immovable.

The Rune of SIG (⚡) outside the Runic circle (⊘)
Primary meaning: you must continue to wait.
Subsidiary meanings: it is necessary to carry on, remain, still – passing time, being dormant, inactive, inert, looking on, wait and see, procrastinating, not progressing, at slack water.

8

TIU'S EIGHT

TIU

This Rune governs *INTRIGUES*.

Key words include: underhand plotting, secret amour, employ secret influence, rouse the interest or curiosity of.

The Rune of TIU (↑) in SKJEBNE (◻)
Primary meaning: completion of project.
Subsidiary meanings: conclusion, end of the matter, maturity, readiness, culmination, climax, summit, achievement, *fait accompli*, finished product, executed, discharged, realized.
Plan, scheme, design, programme of work, policy, strategy, undertaking, engagement, obligation, matter in hand, business venture, promise, enterprise, goal, ambition.

The Rune of TIU (↑) outside SKJEBNE (▢)
Primary meaning: new beginnings.
Subsidiary meanings: not existing before, brought into existence, invented, introduced, discovered, unfamiliar, further, additional, lately arrived, modern, recent, newfangled, not worn or exhausted, fresh, original, not yet accustomed.
Start, set about, time when something starts, openings, channels, opportunities, chances, pastures new, fresh avenues, new fields of experience/work, fresh starts, another chance.

The Rune of TIU (↑) in the Air quadrant (Ⲫ)
Primary meaning: hopes now need action.
Subsidiary meanings: at the present time, this moment, immediately, expectations, presumptions, aspirations, beliefs, ambitions, goals,

visions, dreams, wishes, secret desires.
Require, what is called for, necessary, wanted, lacking, missing,
demanded, claimed, stipulated, ordered.
Performance, doing, transaction, dispatch, execution, force,
energy, handling, act upon, operation, take steps, attempt, try,
implement.

The Rune of TIU (↑) in the Earth quadrant (ᛒ)
Primary meaning: show feelings more.
Subsidiary meanings: reveal, divulge, disclose, express, present,
be unreserved, open, candid, exhibit, expose to view – emotions,
sensations, sympathy, understanding, sentiment, impressions,
passions, desires, needs; don't hide things, keep back, bottle up,
show feelings to a greater degree, extent.

The Rune of TIU (↑) in the Water quadrant (◇)
Primary meaning: when you have what you want – move on.
Subsidiary meanings: when you – possess, have at your disposal,
obtain, get, achieve, succeed, experience, reach – what you –
require, desire, need, are without, lacking, wish for, strive after,
work for, seek after, search for, aspire to, covet, it is the time to –
change, go on, advance, try something else, progress, aim higher,
set things into motion again, be ready to roll, start again, travel,
transpose.

The Rune of TIU (↑) in the Fire quadrant (ᚱ)
Primary meaning: new ways to be tried.
Subsidiary meanings: not existing before, brought into existence,
invented, introduced, discovered, unfamiliar, further additional,
lately arrived, modern, recent, newfangled, fresh, original, not
yet accustomed to.
Potentials, methods, styles, fashions, avenues, doors, openings,
procedures, techniques, routes.
To be tested, examined, sampled, experienced, experimented
with, explored, sounded out, practised, verified, researched,
analysed, inquired into.

The Rune of TIU (↑) outside the Runic circle (∅)
Primary meaning: danger of excess and losing control of the
situation.
Subsidiary meanings: tendency to, liable, likelihood, probability,

good chance, to be expected, forseeable, show signs, in the making, by all odds;
of overdoing things, going over the top, exaggerating, overacting, magnifying, straining, taking on too much, running riot, going to extremes;
by so doing becoming inert, disorganized, impotent, have no say, no grip, no drive, chaos, powerless, incapable of controlling what's going on, circumstances, environment, factors, appearance.

BIRCA ᛒ

This Rune governs *HOME*.

Key words include: where you live with your family, personal life, where you abide, inhabit, carry out your life from, refuge, where you feel comfortable and at ease.

The Rune of BIRCA (ᛒ) in SKJEBNE (◻)
Primary meaning: unity.
Subsidiary meanings: formed into a unit, joined together, become one, combined, consolidated, amalgamated, in agreement, co-operative, harmonious, oneness, absoluteness, whole together, act as one.

The Rune of BIRCA (ᛒ) outside SKJEBNE (▣)
Primary meaning: family gatherings.
Subsidiary meanings: get togethers, meetings, counsel of war, gathering of the clan, relatives, brothers, sisters, parents, aunts, uncles, cousins, in-laws, husbands, wives, the whole tribe, anniversaries, weddings, funerals, christenings, birthday parties, Christmas reunions.

The Rune of BIRCA (ᛒ) in the Air quadrant (ᚣ)
Primary meaning: news of a marriage or a birth.
Subsidiary meanings: information, hear about, be told of; mention of: a wedding, church ceremony, registry office, engagement with a wedding in the offing, handfasting;
beginning of a new life, baby being born, offspring, new beginning, arrival of the stork.

The Rune of BIRCA (ᛒ) in the Earth quadrant (ᛒ)
Primary meaning: regain energy.
Subsidiary meanings: decelerate, don't overdo things, take on too much, ease up, put on the brakes, recharge batteries, shorten sail, reduce speed, rein in, check, curb, back-pedal;
give yourself a chance to revive, pick up, rally, come round, recover, get well, recuperate, return to normal, make a comeback, sleep it off, become yourself again.

The Rune of BIRCA (ᛒ) in the Water quadrant (◇)
Primary meaning: look to the long-term and safeguard legally.
Subsidiary meanings: watch out for, be aware of, regard to, attend to, take notice of, keep an eye on, remember;
long duration, future, permanence, long standing, security, not now but in years to come, future generations, remainder;
make provision, stipulations, protect, precautions –
which are: official, binding, based on or within the province of the law.

The Rune of BIRCA (ᛒ) in the Fire quadrant (ᚱ)
Primary meaning: attend to small detail.
Subsidiary meanings: pay attention, notice, regard, take heed, keep an eye on, application, take pains, concentrate, take care of, find time for, watch;
seemingly insignificant matters, be exact, precise, thorough, right to the last detail, careful, diligent, meticulous, check and recheck, take pains, an eye to detail, minutely, take heed, care, be fastidious.

The Rune of BIRCA (ᛒ) outside the Runic circle (⊘)
Primary meaning: unwanted pregnancy/miscarriage.
Subsidiary meanings: not needed, too many, last straw, burden, parenthood, conception, produced in shame, outside marriage, at an inopportune time, in the family way, carrying, call into being;
stillborn, abort, premature, lose the baby, induced abortion.

EH ᛖ

This Rune governs *CHANGES*.

Key words include: changes of opinion, tastes, reforms, character, turn upside-down, alterations, substitution, differences, new situations, the familiar becomes different.

The Rune of EH (M) in SKJEBNE (□)

Primary meaning: completion of plans.

Subsidiary meanings: conclusion, end of the matter, result, issue, maturity, consummation, executed, discharged, achieved, accomplished, seen through, all ends tied up, clinched, finished off, disposed of.

Schemes, designs, schedules, programmes, arrangements, policies, what you wanted to do, achieve, attain, goals, work towards, strive for.

The Rune of EH (M) outside SKJEBNE (◎)

Primary meaning: love one-sided.

Subsidiary meanings: uneven, by one party only, friendship, affection, tenderness and fondness which is not shared, love-hate, infatuation, a crush, calf-love, an idol, heart-throb, only out for what they can get, being used.

The Rune of EH (M) in the Air quadrant (⋎)

Primary meaning: transitory love.

Subsidiary meanings: not permanent, fading, passing, for the time being only, short and sweet, short-lived, cursory, fleeting, doomed, momentary, not enduring, easy come – easy go, temporary, here today and gone tomorrow, an affair, flirtation, intrigue, light relief.

The Rune of EH (M) in the Earth quadrant (ß)

Primary meaning: new friendship.

Subsidiary meanings: recent, novel, the latest, budding, not existing before, fresh starting, coming into existence, embarking upon, entering into, cropping up;

amity, compatibility, intimacy, relationship, warmth, companion, on good terms, inseparable, close, thick as thieves, loyal, fast, firm.

The Rune of EH (M) in the Water quadrant (◇)

Primary meaning: caution – but appear bold.

Subsidiary meanings: watchfulness, keep watch, hold back a little, don't be too forthcoming, care, heed, vigilance, don't show your hand, don't rush in, watch –

but seem to be by your behaviour; look to be aggressive, red-blooded, daring, adventurous, hardy, audacious, venturesome, ready for anything, unflinching, fearless, intrepid, unshakeable, brave, full of fight, spirited.

The Rune of EH (M) in the Fire quadrant (⌐).
Primary meanings: reveal nothing.
Subsidiary meanings: do not disclose, communicate, leak, give away, confess, let on, indicate, admit, expose, show, unveil, blurt out, spill the beans, come clean, confide, betray, report, tell anybody, not a soul, don't let on, keep quiet, mum, to yourself, secret, hold back, don't reveal anything.

The Rune of EH (M) outside the Runic circle (∅)
Primary meaning: foolish mistakes.
Subsidiary meanings: unthinking, brainless, moronic, stupid, careless, wanting, crass, idiotic, not clever, trifling, fatuous, pointless, purile, conceited, vain;
errors, blunders, misjudgements, miscalculations, inexact, bad ideas, loose thinking, sloppy, off-target, do the wrong thing, slip-ups, clumsy.

MAN ᛗ

This Rune governs *COMMUNICATIONS*.

Key words include: information, transmission of knowledge, news.

The Rune of MAN (ᛗ) in SKJEBNE (□)
Primary meaning: experiment with caution.
Subsidiary meanings: test, try, put to the proof, by guess and God, analyse, get the feel of, branch out, venture, practice upon, research – with care; mindfully, with heed, be on guard, beware, sharp-eyed, pay attention to detail, do your homework, be thorough, meticulous, prepare your groundwork carefully.

The Rune of MAN (ᛗ) outside SKJEBNE (▣)
Primary meaning: contract problems due to lack of communication – do not delegate.
Subsidiary meanings: doubts or difficulties, things hard to

understand, sort out; in connection with mutual agreements between two parties, business agreements, legal documents, marriages. Because of the absence of or a deficiency in speech, transmission of ideas, expression of feelings.

You must not deputize, send a representative or agent, pass on authority; but do things for yourself, don't let someone else do them for you.

The Rune of MAN (ᛗ *) in the Air quadrant (* ᚡ *)*
Primary meaning: reasonableness is called for.
Subsidiary meanings: practice moderation, control, keep in check, keep within bounds, be calm, don't get agitated, expect too much, be fair minded, hold the scales evenly. This is what is required, wanted, needed, essential, a must, a requisite.

The Rune of MAN (ᛗ *) in the Earth quadrant (* ᛒ *)*
Primary meaning: Health hazard caused by strain.
Subsidiary meanings: If you wish to remain fighting fit, have a good constitution, have health and strength, vitality, fitness, good condition, bloom, well-being, be sound as a bell, robust –
do not take chances which cause danger, take risks, overdo things, get tired and fatigued, push yourself to the limit of endurance, or these will bring about the opposite effect.

The Rune of MAN (ᛗ *) in the Water quadrant (* ◇ *)*
Primary meaning: circumstances are against you – whispers.
Subsidiary meanings: you are propelled without resistance, other influences contrast with your own wishes, opposition, collision course.
Insinuations, rumours, secret hints, gossip, slander, scandal, undercurrents, soft rustlings.

The Rune of MAN (ᛗ *) in the Fire quadrant (* ᚠ *)*
Primary meaning: in-depth relationship now develops after the real intent is hidden.
Subsidiary meanings: with a deeper meaning, not just physical, intellectual understanding, far reaching, rapport, regard, affinity, alliance, liaison, twin souls.
Increases, becomes clear, enlarges, expands, matures, blossoms, builds up, widens.
After the real intention, purpose, pursuit, object, goal, design, meaning, aim, context, idea has been concealed, disguised,

veiled, kept secret, not confessed, unnamed, glossed over, bottled up.

The Rune of MAN (ᛗ) outside the Runic circle (⊘)
Primary meaning: untrustworthy.
Subsidiary meanings: doubtful, dubious, uncertain, vague, anybody's guess, treacherous, unpredictable, unreliable, unsure, chancy, risky, unstable, shady, slippery customer, untried, untested, have a suspicion, crooked, scoundrel, rascal, criminal, dishonest, underhand, unfaithful, corrupt.

LAGU ᛚ

This Rune governs *THE EMOTIONS*.

Key words include: feelings, sensations, senses, perception, experience, passions, hopes and fears, affecting your inner self.

The Rune of LAGU (ᛚ) in SKJEBNE (◻)
Primary meaning: psychic powers lead, but know your limits.
Subsidiary meanings: your subconscious, perception, reasoning power, ideas, conceptions, thoughts, from your soul, heart; these serve to direct, point the way, command, spur you on, set the pace.
Take care not to overreach yourself, take on too much, bite off more than you can chew, do only what you know you can safely cope with, know when to draw the line.

The Rune of LAGU (ᛚ) outside SKJEBNE (▣)
Primary meaning: answers found within yourself: outside influences mislead.
Subsidiary meanings: Solutions, the key to the matter, the right course of action will be found in your own mind, is for you to bring out, search for, conceive, formulate.
Situations, monetary problems, responsibilities, commitments, other people's opinions will cloud the issue, give the wrong slant, colour your decision, deceive.

The Rune of LAGU (ᛚ) in the Air quadrant (ᛦ)
Primary meaning: physical attraction will cloud the issue: seek deeper understanding.

Subsidiary meanings: attractions – of the body not of the mind, on the surface, externally, bodily, sensual will:
colour your decision, give the wrong slant, deceive, give a false picture, pull the wool over your eyes.
It will be necessary to dig deeper, fathom out on a different level, look below the surface, probe, enquire, plumb, seek within in order to see through, find the real meaning, gain knowledge.

The Rune of LAGU (⌐) in the Earth quadrant (ꞵ)

Primary meaning: rise above personalities to see.
Subsidiary meanings: look for other meanings and depths that may be hidden by outward appearances, don't be blinded by traits, features, idiosyncracies, qualities, peculiarities, identities, mannerisms.
These will not help you to see matters in depth, to understand, comprehend, recognize, know, discern, make out, grasp: following these will only deceive and take you in.

The Rune of LAGU (⌐) in the Water quadrant (◇)

Primary meaning: darkness; do not stop, feel your way.
Subsidiary meanings: ignorance, unawareness, lack of knowledge, unknown quantities, you are unenlightened, in the dark, uncertain, have nothing to do, but you must:
continue, keep going, persist, carry on, follow through, don't waver or hesitate. Sound things out, be tentative, grope, fumble, get the feel of things, probe, venture, explore, prospect, keep trying.

The Rune of LAGU (⌐) in the Fire quadrant (⌐)

Primary meaning: a more positive approach is called for. Look to the past.
Subsidiary meanings: a new method of attack, way of doing things, style, manner, *modus operandi* is needed, which must be sure, self-confident, unquestionable, know all the answers.
Base this on knowledge and experience already gained, learn from past mistakes, remember what has gone before, earlier happenings, look to your roots.

The Rune of LAGU (⌐) outside the Runic circle (∅)

Primary meaning: don't be sidetracked by opposition.
Subsidiary meanings: don't be disorientated, misdirected, take the wrong course, go off at a tangent, be led astray, put off the scent, held back by –

antagonism, hindrance, interference, opposing causes, non-co-operation rivalry, resistance, protests, obstacles, obstructions; you must make a stand and stick to your guns.

ING ◇

This Rune governs affecting *DIRECT FAMILY*.

Key words include: close relations, wife/husband, parents, children, brothers, sisters, aunts, uncles, etc.

The Rune of ING (◇) in SKJEBNE (□)
Primary meaning: change leading to improvement.
Subsidiary meanings: difference, variation, alteration, fresh phase, substitution, something new, not routine;
causing, bringing about, directly responsible for, inspiring, originating from, resulting in, bringing to pass, sparking off, provoking: progress, forward motion, betterment, advance, showing promise, make strides, headway, development, further-ance, gain, achievement.

The Rune of ING (◇) outside SKJEBNE (▣)
Primary meaning: move of home.
Subsidiary meanings: change of residence, new environment, new surroundings, fresh place to live, new roots, pastures new, beginnings, adventure, new faces, different house.

The Rune of ING (◇) in the Air quadrant (Ⱶ)
Primary meaning: change your plans – be versatile and giving.
Subsidiary meanings: differ, vary, alter, substitute, something new, project, schemes, designs, undertakings, ventures, engage-ments, programme of work, strategy.
What is needed is: elasticity, be prepared to handover, variety, readiness, ease, become many-sided, faceted.

The Rune of ING (◇) in the Earth quadrant (ᛒ)
Primary meaning: personal attitude must show change.
Subsidiary meanings: your own, private, no one else's, individual, way of thinking, behaviour, point of view, way of judgement, reasoning, reactions, thoughts;
have to be seen to alter, vary, become different, a new angle, a new slant.

The Rune of ING (◇ *) in the Water quadrant (* ◇ *)*
Primary meaning: outside influences lead to change.
Subsidiary meanings: events beyond your control, out of your power, another person's actions, something in which you have no sway, authority over, force of circumstances, general state of affairs, fate, destiny;
cause, bring about, are responsible for, result in, spark off, provoke, bring to pass, underlie, found –
a difference, variation, alteration, something new, substitution, not routine, new angle, new slant.

The Rune of ING (◇ *) in the Fire quadrant (* ⌐ *)*
Primary meaning: your actions to benefit another.
Subsidiary meanings: your own, personal, private, individual, no one else's – movements, doings, energy, influence, steps taken, deeds, functions, chosen course;
will be to the advantage of, do good to, bring privilege to, help, assist, profit, aid – someone else, not you, some other person.

The Rune of ING (◇ *) outside the Runic circle (* ∅ *)*
Primary meaning: misrepresentations.
Subsidiary meanings: represent wrongly, give false account of, false light, travesty, parody, caricature, distorted image, misinformation, over-dramatized, exaggerated account, be false, detract, toned down, bumped up.

ODAL ⊗

This Rune governs *MOUNTAINS TO CLIMB.*

Key words include: obstacles to be overcome, scaled, risen above, work one's way up, struggle up, ascend from bottom of the ladder.

The Rune of ODAL (⊗ *) in SKJEBNE (* □ *)*
Primary meaning: gain from own effort.
Subsidiary meanings: getting, winning, acquiring, thrift, savings, profit, earn a dividend, succeed, make money, come by, reap, increase;
brought about: personally, not by another, independently, unaided, in private, on your own;

and by your own: exertion, struggles, drive, force, energy, muscle, work, labour, perseverence.

The Rune of ODAL (✕) outside SKJEBNE (▢)
Primary meaning: legacy/property buying or selling difficulties.
Subsidiary meanings: inheritance, possessions, chattels, belongings, estate, birthright, heritage, bequest, moveables, effects, assets.
Obstacles requiring effort to be removed, embarrassment, objections, awkward situations, problems, worries, hurdles, stumbling blocks;
concerned with exchanging for money, purchasing, procuring or disposing of, finding a purchaser, trading in, making over.

The Rune of ODAL (✕) in the Air quadrant (⋎)
Primary meaning: the need is a willing sacrifice.
Subsidiary meanings: what is called for, requirement, necessary, missing, demanded, claimed, stipulated, ordered –
is a: voluntary, spontaneous, consenting, ready acquiescence, of free will, with a good grace, nothing loth, gladly, with pleasure, happy;
surrender, offering, victim, devotion, resign oneself, giving up something for the sake of another.

The Rune of ODAL (✕) in the Earth quadrant (ß)
Primary meaning: strength given for the climb up.
Subsidiary meanings: capacity to bear, reinforcement, power, energy, courage, will power, guts, potency, might, tolerance, support, perseverance, fight, what it takes;
is bestowed, presented, donated, granted, conferred, invested, vouchsafed, provided –
for the ascent, struggle up, rise, take off, climbing the ladder, try for the top, upward motion, upsurge.

The Rune of ODAL (✕) in the Water quadrant (◇)
Primary meaning: now you must dare – expand.
Subsidiary meanings: at the present time, this moment, immediately, you are obliged, commanded, have no choice, the only course open, it is imperative, a necessary move;
attempt, exert yourself, take a chance, venture, speculate, gamble, have a go, do;
broaden, widen, stretch out, stretch yourself, extend, unfold, throw off reserve, increase, extend trade, territory, new horizons,

new avenues, greater scope and understanding.

The Rune of ODAL (⋈) in the Fire quadrant (⌐)
Primary meaning: determination wins.
Subsidiary meanings: resolution, a sticking point, earnestness,
seriousness, resolve, decision, being intent upon, endurance,
carry through, stand no nonsense, will power, resolve, tenacity,
concentration, single mindedness, constancy, grit, courage;
will mean: a happy ending, success story, time well spent,
triumph, accomplishment, pays dividends, victory, fruitless,
unbeaten, make the grade, pull it off, arrive, achieve mastery.

The Rune of ODAL (⋈) outside the Runic circle (⊘)
Primary meaning: beware of moving wheels.
Subsidiary meanings: caution, be warned, take care, pay heed,
mind out for, danger signal, hint, forewarned, be on your guard,
be prepared;
wheels in motion, wheels within wheels, a puzzle, clockwork,
machinery, wheel of fate turning; might be an accident concerned
with wheels, a car, train, bicycle, machine.

DAG ⋈

This Rune governs *AMBITION*.

Key words include: hopes, expectations, aspirations, visions,
dreams, desires, goals, what one strives for/towards, intentions,
pursuits, targets, have in mind.

The Rune of DAG (⋈) in SKJEBNE (□)
Primary meaning: effort rewarded.
Subsidiary meanings: measures, steps taken, something done,
performed, executed, implemented, administered, laboured at,
exertion, stress, strain, trouble, employment, hard work, do one's
utmost, keep at it; pays off, brings prestige, remuneration,
compensation, thanks, profit, just desserts, compliments, honours,
has not gone unnoticed, brings repute, acknowledgement.

The Rune of DAG (⋈) outside SKJEBNE (▣)
Primary meaning: be positive in a negative situation.
Subsidiary meanings: be certain, sure, confident, convinced,

reliable, steadfast, unquestionable, undeniable, guaranteed – in circumstances, environment, predicaments which seem to express or imply denial, prohibitive, unsuccessful, frustrating, losing battle, profitless, abortive; don't let them grind you down.

The Rune of DAG (ᛞ) in the Air quadrant (ᚨ)
Primary meaning: stay your hand.
Subsidiary meanings: delay, wait and see, play for time, postpone, adjourn, procrastinate, hold back, put off, shelve, temporize, stall, hold in abeyance, keep your plans secret, don't be too open, forthcoming.

The Rune of DAG (ᛞ) in the Earth quadrant (ᛒ)
Primary meaning: make advances where you can.
Subsidiary meanings: make progress, take steps forward, gain headway, steal a march, gain, develop, achieve, make ground, forge ahead, move up, surge forward;
when able, at every opportunity, opening, every chance, whenever possible, use what comes to hand, within your grasp.

The Rune of DAG (ᛞ) in the Water quadrant (◇)
Primary meaning: action seen to be in progress.
Subsidiary meanings: movements, doings, energy, influence, steps taken, deeds, functions, chosen course;
apparently, visibly, noticeably, by the look of it, observable, manifesting, happening, appearing, actually, perceptibly, recognizable, happening, being done, making headway, evolving, coming about, going on, occurring, becoming, taking place, the order of the day.

The Rune of DAG (ᛞ) in the Fire quadrant (ᛚ)
Primary meaning: a new and better lifestyle.
Subsidiary meanings: not existing before, brought into existence, invented, introduced, unfamiliar, fresh, improved, of a more excellent kind, surpassing what has gone before, change for the better;
existence, way of living, nature, improved standard of living, manner of existence.

The Rune of DAG (ᛞ) outside the Runic circle (∅)
Primary meaning: effort unrecognized.
Subsidiary meanings: measures, steps taken, something done,

performance, executed, implemented, labour, exertion, stress, strain, trouble, employment, hard work, struggles, do one's utmost, keep at it;

no word of praise, not rewarded, labour of love, unsung, ignored, forgotten, unnoticed, glossed over, no word of thanks, without payment.

9

SKJEBNE

This Rune governs *DESTINY*.

Key words include: kismet, one's lot, predestination, fortune, destiny, in the stars, god's will, prescribed course.

The Rune of SKJEBNE (☐ *) in SKJEBNE (* ☐ *)*
Primary meaning: that which must be accepted.
Subsidiary meanings: that which must be tolerated, put up with, the inevitable, fate, destiny, fortune, gone along with, no choice in the matter, out of your hands, conform to, in the stars, one's lot, foreordained.

The Rune of SKJEBNE (☐ *) outside SKJEBNE (* ▣ *)*
Primary meaning: a problem that must now be faced.
Subsidiary meanings: difficulty, predicament, quandry, cornered, complication, trouble, worry, difficult situation, headache, enigma, concern, something hard to handle, a burden, fly in the ointment;
must now be dealt with, recognized, handled, sorted out, not left unsolved any longer, tackled, owned up to.

The Rune of SKJEBNE (☐ *) in the Air quadrant (* ⼂ *)*
Primary meaning: you meet your match.
Subsidiary meanings: you come up against someone just like you, your twin soul, doppelganger, your double, someone just as crafty, same personality, cannot be bettered, one jump ahead, equal, corresponding exactly, up to all your own tricks.

The Rune of SKJEBNE (☐ *) in the Earth quadrant (* ᛒ *)*
Primary meaning: a price to pay.

Subsidiary meanings: not something for nothing, a penalty, account to settle, levy, face the music, forfeit, pay the costs, damages, compensation, return favour, as you sow so shall you reap, come-uppance, settle up, reckoning, make an example, lesson to learn.

The Rune of SKJEBNE (□) in the Water quadrant (◇)
Primary meaning: the situation is not in your hands.
Subsidiary meanings: circumstances, what is going on, environment, lay of the land, predicament, position, prevailing conditions – not in your control, unmanageable, intractable, not your decision, down to someone else, brought about by outside influences, in the lap of the gods, in the air.

The Rune of SKJEBNE (□) in the Fire quadrant (┌)
Primary meaning: you succeed.
Subsidiary meanings: happy ending, success story, triumph, fruitful, undefeated, make the grade, accomplish, achieve, reach your goal, show results, hit the jackpot, arrive, graduate, qualify, make out, pull it off, make a breakthrough, do marvels, bear fruit.

The Rune of SKJEBNE (□) outside the Runic circle (∅)
Primary meaning: a necessary failure.
Subsidiary meanings: no alternative, had to happen, no choice, force of circumstances, required, unforgoable, indespensable, unavoidable, fated, imposed;
faux pas, blunder, error, non-event, mistake, miscalculation, slip-up, wrong idea, clanger, oversight, mistiming.

BIBLIOGRAPHY

ARBMAN, Holger *The Vikings* (Thames & Hudson).

BRANSTON, Brian *The Lost Gods of England* (Thames & Hudson).

BUTLER, Bill *The Definitive Tarot* (Rider & Co.).

CARLYON, Richard *A Guide to the Gods* (William Heinemann Ltd.).

CAVENDISH, Richard *Encyclopedia of The Unexplained* (Routledge & Kegan Paul).

CROWLEY, Aleister *The Book of Thoth* (Samuel Weiser Inc.).

DIRINGER, David *The Alphabet* (Hutchinson).

ELLIOTT, R.W.V. *Runes* (Manchester University Press).

ELLIS-DAVIDSON, H. R. *Scandinavian Mythology* (Hamlyn).

GRAVES, Robert *The White Goddess* (Faber & Faber).

GRIMAL, Pierre *Larousse World Mythology* (Hamlyn).

NICOLSON, James R. *Shetland Folklore* (Robert Hale).

PAGE, R. L. *An Introduction to English Runes* (Methuen).

SMITH, Christine *The Book of Divination* (Rider & Co.).

TAYLOR, Paul B. and AUDEN, W. H. *The Elder Edda: A Selection* (Faber & Faber).

TURVILLE-PETRE, E. O. G. *Myth and Religion of the North* (Weidenfeld & Nicolson).

VALIENTE, Doreen *Witchcraft for Tomorrow* (Robert Hale Ltd.).

VARLEY, Desmond *Seven the Number of Creation* (G. Bell & Sons).

Encyclopaedia Britannica (William Benton).

SUPPLIERS

Wooden Runes – Boxed
Michael Westgate
The Old School
16 The Street
GELDESTON
Norfolk

Porcelain & Terracotta Runes and Casting Cloths
Mrs Viki Burke
The Old Post Office
Antiques & Pottery
Blofield
NORWICH
Norfolk

INDEX

alchemy, 24
alphabet, 14, 18
    Hebrew, 30
Aquizi, 70-2

Birca, 76-7
brooch, Hunterston, 21

calendars, perpetual, 19
Casket, Frank's, 21
Clog almanacs, 19
crosses, 21
currency, (£sd), 21

Dag, 86-8
destiny, 23

Eh, 77-9
Elder Edda, The, 16

Feoh, 48-9
Freya's Eight, 15
Futhork, 15

Gifu, 58-9

Hagal's Eight, 15
Hanged Man, the, 26
Hippocrates, 26

I Ching, 9, 29
Ing, 83-4
Is, 64-5

Jung, Carl, 9

Kaon, 56-8
karma, 22

Lagu, 81-3

Man, 79-81

Naut, 62-4
Nazis, 19
Nostradamus, 7
numerology, 26, 29

Odal, 84-6
Odin, 16, 17, 26, 28, 29
Oss, 53-5

Peorth, 69-70
Primstaves, runic, 19

Rit, 55
ritual, 10
Roman Church, 18
runa, 14

runes, 19
  casting, 22
  groups of, 31
runic characters, 9, 14, 16
  cloth, 27
  inscriptions, 21

Scandinavia, 16
Sig, 72-3
skjebne, 22, 25, 89
Sleipnir, 17
symbols, 14
synchronistic events, 9

Tarot, 9, 18, 29

Thorn, 51-3
Tiu, 74-6
Tiu's Eight, 15

Ur, 49-51
Urunnen, 19

Volsunga Saga, 11

Will o' the Wisp, 8
Wunna, 59-61

Yer, 65-7
Yggdrasil, 16, 29
Yr, 67-8